B D1460037

This book is due for return on or before the last date
shown above but it may be renewed unless required
by other readers, by personal application, post, or
telephone, quoting this date and the author and title.

VIEW OF
THE CHILTERNS

VIEW OF
THE CHILTERNS

Written and photographed by

BRIAN J. BAILEY

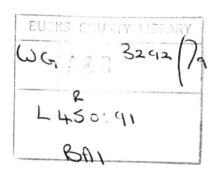
ROBERT HALE · LONDON

Other books by Brian J. Bailey

Portrait of Leicestershire
Portrait of Hertfordshire

Other books in the View Series

View of Devon
View of Sussex
View of Wessex
View of Yorkshire

© *Brian J. Bailey 1979*
First published in Great Britain 1979

ISBN 0 7091 7684 8

Robert Hale Limited
Clerkenwell House
Clerkenwell Green
London, EC1

Photoset, printed and bound
in Great Britain by
REDWOOD BURN LIMITED
Trowbridge and Esher

Frontispiece: The Turville valley.

CONTENTS

LIST OF ILLUSTRATIONS

To
MY WIFE –
my accessory before,
during and after
the fact

INTRODUCTION

"I see you are writing about the Chilterns, young man." (She is entitled to refer to the middle forties as young, since she is a lady considerably advanced in years.) *"If you expect me to buy the book, you had better tell me how it differs from others on the subject."*

"I hardly know, madam, since I have not yet written it, but let us see if I can whet your appetite.

"The Chilterns are one of the oldest of English families, residing mainly in Buckinghamshire, Oxfordshire and Hertfordshire but with close relations in Bedfordshire and Berkshire. They cannot trace their ancestry back as far as the Cheviots of Northumberland; nor have they achieved the lofty status of the Pennines of Yorkshire. They have neither the hidden depths of the Mendips of Somerset nor the showy conceit of the Cotswolds of Gloucestershire. They are a quiet and unassuming family, whose daughters are modest beauties of the nicest English type, with soft curves and fair complexions. To be in their company is always a pleasure."

"There's no need to adopt that mawkish tone with me, young man! I may be old, but I'm not one of your foolish Victorian spinsters."

"Forgive me: I used the analogy only to establish at the outset that the Chilterns are a close-knit group with the same blood running through their veins, as it were, and that the artificial divisions of the county boundaries will be used only as a convenient way of separating the text into chapters."

"Very well. But I hope it's not going to be one of those books that go on and on about golden saxifrage and wild orchids. What is your special interest? Geology, ornithology or botany?"

"Alas, no, madam. I confess my chief interest is in humanity."

"Indeed! I am pleased to hear it. There are too many books filled with facts today. Facts lie thick on the ground for anyone to pick up, and they

quite suffocate the imagination. Humanity necessarily entails speculation, since Man knows everything but his own mind. But why, in that case, have you picked on the Chilterns? Are you not aware that they have always been a sparsely populated area?"

"But also a den of thieves and witches; a retreat for outlaws; the scene of orgies; a hide-out for heretics."

"Then for goodness sake get on with it, young man, and you may put me down for a copy. But make sure it is not delivered to the tradesmen's entrance. It would never do for the servants to read it!"

ACKNOWLEDGMENTS

The chief printed works on which I have relied are listed at the end of the book, but I have to express my gratitude to all those people, too numerous to mention individually, who helped by answering my queries or by permitting me to take photographs. In particular, I must acknowledge the co-operation of the Trustees of the Bedford Estates, who allowed me to see and photograph the Bedford Chapel at Chenies.

I am heavily indebted to my friends Van Phillips and Kenneth Scowen for their helpful advice, but at the same time – conscious that the result must fall short of their high literary and artistic standards – I am anxious to absolve them from any responsibility for the book's inadequacies.

My incalculable debt to my wife is inadequately conveyed in the dedication.

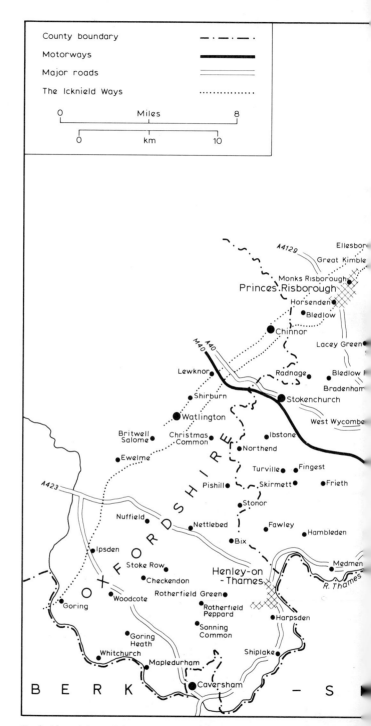

CHAPTER I

THE SECRET CHILTERNS

THE CHILTERN HILLS form the northern rim of a giant saucer, in the middle of which lies London – the cup that overfloweth. The hills are part of a continuous belt of chalk running in a north-easterly direction from the coast of Dorset to the coast of Norfolk, being then broken by the Wash before continuing along the coast of Yorkshire. The chalk was formed (according to the geological faith) during the Cretaceous period, about a hundred million years ago, and was then beneath the sea. It is a porous white limestone formed largely from planktonic algae and the shells of tiny sea-creatures, and it often contains a large amount of flint in the upper layer. Most Chiltern churches are built of this material.

The romantic interpretation would be that the Chilterns rose, white and virginal, out of the sea like Aphrodite, but it would be more suggestive of their character to say that they remained under wraps long after most of Britain had been exposed.

However, if my brief introduction and the present chapter-heading have led any reader, unfamiliar with the Chilterns, to think they are a kind of elevated Sherwood Forest, let me correct that impression at once. As well as having great natural beauty, the Chilterns embrace one of England's richest funeral treasure-houses, one of its oldest surviving theatres, one of its rarest church towers, its highest artificial watercourse and its oldest free Church of England school, to say nothing of the world's largest

In Burnham Beeches. Owned by the Corporation of the City of London, Burnham Beeches is a public open space between Slough and Beaconsfield, containing the largest collection of ancient beeches in the world.

collection of ancient beeches. Yet it is true to say that the Chilterns remain secretive and reticent.

The one single – and singular – factor which has most dictated the whole history and appearance of the Chiltern Hills has been the absence of water, the first necessity of life. You have only to pick up any one of those calendars of Enchanting England, Wondrous Wales or Staggering Scotland to see at once that the proportion of photographs in this book with water in them is very low indeed, and of those I *have* included, the majority is of the Thames or of village ponds that were probably artificial in origin.

Reflections of trees and buildings in the mirror-like surfaces of placid lakes, and great rivers tumbling over granite-like boulders, are not here to be photographed. Where there were moated homesteads, the moats were dry, and the only limpid pools were those with ornamental goldfish in them, created by landscape gardeners by damming the trickling streams that occur here and there. The scarcity of surface water may well have affected the very build and complexion of the people. Cobbett remarked that the girls of High Wycombe were "somewhat larger featured and larger boned than those of Sussex, and not so fresh-coloured and bright-eyed". And they were not factory-workers, shop-assistants and shorthand-typists – permanently shut up indoors – in those days.

The natural springs were sufficient for the nomadic peoples who first trod this way, but the difficulties of obtaining water in quantity, as well as the effect of the chalk soil on agricultural possibilities, were responsible for the sparse settlement in the Chilterns right up to comparatively recent times. We may take it as a rule of thumb that the farther away a village or hamlet is from a natural water supply, the more recent its origin. As wells, communal village pumps and then piped water became available, communities could afford to build their homes further from springs and rivers. Thus the original centres of villages such as Sarratt and Flaunden are always nearer to the water supply than their subsequent extensions or migrations.

The Chilterns have no shortage of rain, of course. It is simply that the chalk soaks it up rapidly. Beneath the ground are extensive natural reservoirs, where water lies on the clay underneath the

Northend pond. This village pond, on the chalk nearly seven hundred feet above sea level, is doubtless artificial in origin, probably having been lined with clay bonded with straw to prevent rainwater soaking away.

chalk, and from these comes most of the mains water for the area. Gardeners aware of the need for well-drained soil do not know what the phrase means until they have done some gardening on chalk. The gardens of large mansions, and the occasional parks, are affected by it, as well as smaller private gardens. When Lancelot Brown was called in to the great Chiltern houses to consider the 'capabilities' of the grounds, one idea that was definitely closed to him was the creation of banks of rhododendron and azalea. The chalk soil is alkaline, except for a belt of acid soil down the eastern edge of the Chilterns of Hertfordshire and Buckinghamshire. There are rhododendrons at Cliveden, and – surprisingly – they can be found growing wild in Burnham Beeches, but they are not of the finest quality.

In turn, the water shortage helped to dictate the lack of a clear Chiltern cultural tradition, the look of farms, fields and hedges, and so on. The only common Chiltern practice was defiance of the rules. This makes the hills all the more attractive, in some ways. Except in rare places of real (and, it must be admitted, artificial) style, such as Amersham and Ewelme, there is none of that instant unity in the village streets that speaks of 'town planning'; nor are there any local gastronomic specialities to be advertised in restaurants and tea-shops. There is no great literature of the Chilterns, nor a common language that could sensibly be described as a Chiltern dialect. No statues to great men ornament the Chiltern streets. Split up by administrative, if not natural, boundaries, and lacking – through scattered and isolated settlement – that close communication which leads to uniformity of habit and outlook, the Chilterns have a splendid diversity linked – in appearance at least – only by the landscape and by use of the available flint in their old buildings.

At any rate, after prehistoric earth movements had raised the chalk above the sea, the dip of the saucer was covered by glacial deposits which are generally known as the London Clay. Through this dip, via one of a series of gaps in the chalk ridge, the River Thames flows, collecting tribute from the surrounding hills during its majestic procession to the capital. The Thames at Goring is the natural southern boundary of the Chilterns. Across the river the Berkshire Downs begin.

Along the north-western boundary of the Chilterns, the escarpment rises steeply from the low ground of southern Oxfordshire and the Vale of Aylesbury, so there is no problem of definition on that side. On the southern and eastern flanks, the hills slope gently down to the Thames valley, and we can reasonably embrace the southern end of Buckinghamshire and the western end of Hertfordshire from around Chorleywood to the Bedfordshire border near Luton. Few would argue with that, I am sure, though it is rather stretching the imagination to include Stoke Poges, which

Gray's Monument, Stoke Poges. This photograph is my sole concession to those who insist that Stoke Poges is in the Chilterns. The monument to the author of 'Elegy in a Country Churchyard' was designed by James Wyatt and erected in 1799. It is in the care of the National Trust.

The Thames at Goring. The point from which the chalk hills rise on both sides of north. The Icknield Way and the Ridgeway

the Thames — the Berkshire Downs to the south and the Chiltern Hills to the
were joined by a ford across the river.

hardly any writer on the Chilterns seems able to resist, on account of its association with Gray's 'Elegy'.

The northern Chilterns cause most difficulty in defining their extent. It is certainly true that the ridge is continuous along the Bedfordshire and Hertfordshire border as far as Hitchin, and it may be technically correct to say that the Chilterns run beyond Royston and into Cambridgeshire and Suffolk, to merge with the Gog Magog Hills and what are whimsically called the East Anglian Heights. However, the family relations residing beyond Royston are of doubtful lineage, and even those beyond Luton are of inferior character. From the points of view of the tourist and the walking enthusiast, as opposed to those of the geologist and the geographer, the Chilterns effectively end at Dunstable Downs. Stopping my ears against the outcry of purists, therefore, I propose to regard the Chilterns, for the purposes of this book, as stretching about thirty-eight miles on a north-east axis from Goring in Oxfordshire to Dunstable in Bedfordshire.

Furthermore, I intend to reverse the usual procedure by travelling from north to south when I discuss the area in more detail. Almost everyone seems to do the opposite, perhaps due to being London-orientated, but I am a Midlander and do not regard London as the centre of the world. Besides, north to south was the direction in which the first humans penetrated the chalk hills. They were pre-Celtic nomads who crossed the North Sea from the Continent and landed around the Norfolk coast. Following the chalk ridge inland, they must have wandered along these hills, crossed the Thames and progressed to Salisbury Plain, where one of the oldest monuments in Europe, Stonehenge, stands as an enduring witness to their eventual settlement on this island.

The route they followed also became permanent. They used it to travel back and forth, presumably trading across the North Sea, exchanging tin and copper mined in Cornwall for livestock and spices, perhaps, and digging flint from the chalk to make tools for cultivating the thin soil. Grimes' Graves, the flint mine in Norfolk, is on the route of what is possibly one of the oldest roads in western Europe, and certainly the oldest in Britain, the Icknield Way. Along the Chilterns it is divided for much of the way, and on the

The Lower Icknield Way. This part of Britain's most ancient road, near Aston Rowant, is still a pleasant traffic-free green lane, but much of the track is now surfaced and motorized highway.

other side of the Thames it continues as The Ridgeway. It is probable that the more northerly of the Chiltern branches, called 'the Lower Icknield Way' because it is at the foot of the escarpment, is the oldest. The higher route may well have been made to avoid swamps which would have formed in the thick forest in winter.

The attraction of the ridge was that the bare chalk offered a dry and accessible route across country. It would have been comparatively easy to clear for grazing livestock, and water was available from springs which occur where water, lying on the clay beneath the chalk, seeps through the surface. The nomadic people would no doubt have settled here and there along the route, clearing the forest by setting fire to it and raising their crops of grain until the poor thin soil had been exhausted, when they moved on to another site.

Although the Chilterns possess no prehistoric monuments as spectacular as those of Wiltshire, there are signs of neolithic and later activity throughout their length, beginning with Maiden Bower and Five Knolls, near Dunstable – the first of Stone-Age origin but evidently used in the Iron Age as a sort of transit camp rather than a permanent settlement. The Five Knolls are a group of burial mounds. Occasional discoveries of flint tools, bronze axes or ancient coins, as well as the existence of flint mines and Iron-Age hill-forts, indicate the continuing use of the Icknield Way up to the coming of the Romans. The name 'Icknield' is thought by some to be derived from Iceni, the tribe ruled by Boudicca in East Anglia. The name 'Chiltern' itself is of Saxon origin, from 'chilt', meaning chalk. (There is an extraordinary number of place-names beginning with Ch – Chalfont, Chipperfield, Chinnor, Chenies, Chartridge, Chequers, Checkendon, to name but a few; but we must not jump to the wrong conclusion about them. Most are derived from Norman landowners and lords of the manors.)

One curious phenomenon, the chalk figures cut into the hillsides, occurs wherever there are chalk hills and downs in Britain, but particularly on the ridge stretching from Dorset to East Anglia. There is much uncertainty about the origin of most of them, but some prehistoric artist has a lot to answer for, in starting a trend in large-scale design culminating in the white lion at Whipsnade. This marked a departure from the norm in chalk figures, since it is naturalistic, whereas the older carvings are invariably stylized. This lion roars all the vulgarity of modern advertising over a wide area of Bedfordshire and Buckinghamshire.

There are no chalk carvings in the Chilterns to compare with the Uffington White Horse or the Cerne Abbas Giant, but there are two or three which may be as ancient, though their age is much disputed. (It is an interesting curiosity that the designer of the Uffington White Horse might have been left-handed, whereas the designers of the Cerne Abbas man and the Whipsnade lion were certainly right-handed.) All the Chiltern carvings are on the west-facing escarpment, so as to be seen at a distance, though that purpose has now been defeated to some extent by the growth of trees around them. They are symbols rather than figures. They are near Bledlow and Whiteleaf in Buckinghamshire, and Watlington in Oxfordshire, the first two being in the form of crosses on pedestals,

The White Lion, Whipsnade. The most modern of Chiltern chalk figures, it was designed by R. B. Brooke-Greaves and carved in 1932. This view is from Dagnall, but it can be seen clearly from a considerably greater distance.

The Whiteleaf Cross. The largest and most prominent of the chalk carvings is this glorified graffito of unknown age. It is probably not more than three hundred years old.

and the third a sort of obelisk. The largest and clearest is the Whiteleaf Cross, which can be seen over a wide area. It is tempting to regard them all as phallic symbols, but there is no proof that they are really old, and indeed there is no known mention of them earlier than the mid-eighteenth century. They may have been made as a hoax, like Piltdown Man, not so long ago, or they may be ancient symbols turned into crosses by Christians who took exception to their phallic connotation. We must resign ourselves to uncertainty, but it is one of the nicer Chiltern ironies that what may have been the week-end prank of some eighteenth-century students is now preserved as a national monument. *O sancto graffito!*

With the Roman occupation, the pattern of the Chilterns, commenced by nature and altered by Celtic and Belgic farmers, was changed again, and this time the modern aspect began to show itself. Nature had weathered the soft chalk into gently curving hills with dry valleys – what are called 'Wind Gaps' – carved by the receding ice. (Quite unlike the harder carboniferous limestone of the Mendips, where rivers have worn great chasms and gorges in the rock, as at Cheddar.)

"I hope you are not going to suggest, young man, that they are as different as chalk from cheese!"

"Certainly not, madam! Do you take me for a punster?"

Ancient man, following the ridge, found the valleys barriers to his progress and had to negotiate them. From the time of the Romans, however, the hills themselves have been the barriers, and the valleys the lines of least resistance. A glance at the map shows instantly the contrasting approaches of the pre-Roman people and of 'civilized' man since the establishment of London. The Romans drove their military roads, later known as Akeman Street and Watling Street, through the gaps at Tring and Dunstable, and all subsequent major routes through the Chilterns have been in a north-westerly direction out of the capital.

There was no Roman town in the Chilterns farther south than Dunstable, but remains of villas indicate that the heavily wooded hills were regarded as suitable country retreats for the well-to-do, a view that has been in currency, broadly speaking, during the two thousand ensuing years. But the Chilterns remained a thinly populated area due to the poor quality of the chalk soil. Rising to an average height of seven or eight hundred feet, they reach their highest point (852 feet) at Coombe Hill, near Wendover. They are now the most densely wooded hills left in England, and the characteristic vegetation is short springy turf and beech.

A tree so prolific that it probably gave Buckinghamshire its name (from the Old English 'bece'), and which was long ago nicknamed 'the Chiltern weed', obviously demands some attention. *Fagus sylvatica* is, in fact, a ruthless monopolist. Native to southern England, the beech's shallow, spreading roots enable it to thrive on thin soil where many other trees will not grow. Furthermore, its dense foliage prevents all but a little sunlight from reaching the ground beneath it, so it discourages competition, and few plants grow in its shade. Thus the typical beechwood has a floor carpeted with its rich brown and rot-resistant leaves, lit by a little dappled sunlight, and often remarkably still and quiet. Only the silence is more golden than the forest floor. Thrushes, jays and grey squirrels rustle about in the leaves searching for insects and beech-mast – the little brown nuts that fed the swine kept in the woods in medieval times. Beech can live for over two hundred years and may reach a height of over a hundred feet. The smooth grey bark of a healthy tree grown in ideal conditions contrasts mightily with the grotesque shapes of aged trees allowed to go their own ways, or pollarded, and many such strange specimens can be seen in the woods at Ashridge and Burnham Beeches. Beech is the most widely planted deciduous tree today, and in controlled cultivation it forms a long straight trunk whose hard, strong timber has been highly valued in furniture-making for centuries. But that is a Chiltern story in itself, to which we must soon return.

It was natural that such early settlement as took place in these hills should be scattered and form into small villages and hamlets where the forest was cleared by the farmers. A seventh-century Saxon monk had referred (in the first written mention of the hills we know of) to 'the Deserts of Chiltern'. The Saxons preferred to farm the heavy clay soils in the valleys, and it was probably in

Grim's Ditch. This is part of a long stretch of the ditch near Great Hampden. The depression does not appear very great here, but the picture is slightly deceptive. Enormous quantities of earth had to be dug to make the bank on the right.

Saxon times that the beech became rampant on the deserted uplands, though it is thought to have begun its colonization of the chalk two or three thousand years BC. Most of the village names date from after the Norman Conquest, and to this day, although the Chilterns have a few quite large towns round their fringes, there is only one of any size deep in their midst – High Wycombe.

We must not imagine that there were no people in the hills at all, however. Indeed, it seems that one important characteristic of Chiltern folk had been observed within a century of William of Normandy's invasion. According to a famous passage in the *Anglo-Saxon Chronicle*, during the reign of King Stephen: "Then was corn dear and flesh and cheese, for none there was in the land. The wretched people perished with hunger; some, who had been great men, were driven to beggary, while others fled from the country . . . and men said openly that Christ slept, and all his saints." It was at this time that the Stewardship of the Chiltern

30

Hundreds was established. The officer's responsibility was to put an end to the frequent robbery of travellers by the lawless Chiltern inhabitants! This was three and a half centuries before Columbus discovered America. To the citizens of London and eastern England, the Chiltern area was the wild west. To some of them, it still is.

Civilizing influences may have softened 'lawlessness' a bit, but a fierce independence of spirit was recognized as one of the traits of the hill people for centuries after that, and it is ironic that the office, though only a sinecure, still exists.

Sweeping intermittently in a wide arc across the northern Chilterns from near Berkhamsted towards High Wycombe is that mysterious excavation Grim's Ditch, called by Massingham "the longest serpent of antiquity". It probably had its present name bestowed upon it by early Christians who identified Grim (another name for Odin or Woden) with the Devil and could imagine no other creator of such daunting earthworks. (It was certainly not made on a Wednesday!)

Theories abound as to the ditch's origin and purpose, but experts are generally agreed that it is more likely to be of Saxon than of prehistoric date. Its apparent uselessness as a line of defence has led to the assumption that it was a boundary line between the kingdoms of Mercia and Wessex, but I remain sceptical. If it was a boundary line without any defensive or protective purpose, why the toil and sweat of digging so many tons of earth when a line of stakes would have served equally well? And why create an artificial boundary line on a complicated route through the hills (the ditch makes a sharp right-angle turn as it approaches Princes Risborough) when the line of the escarpment itself forms such an obvious natural one? Such an idea could surely only occur to modern men spoon-fed on principles of bureaucracy − ancient men were not so daft.

Does this ditch have any connection with the one of the same name starting twelve miles away, between Nuffield and Nettlebed? And is the line discontinuous because subsequent farming has obliterated much of it, or because it was hurriedly begun and never completed? Its course runs remarkably parallel with the line of the escarpment, and it is curious that the rough semi-circle between Northchurch and The Lee encloses an Iron-Age hill-fort, Cholesbury Camp.

The *Anglo-Saxon Chronicle* records that the Danes made repeated raids in this area in the years 1009 and 1010: '. . . they made an incursion away through the Chilterns, and so came to Oxford, and burned down the borough, and made their way back on both sides of the Thames. . . .' By 1011 the Danes had overrun Buckinghamshire and Oxfordshire, and then a truce was made with them. It is often objected, when the ditch is regarded as a defensive earthwork, that the hollow is on the wrong side of the bank. But if it was a defensive artifact against the Danes, who knows from which direction the next raid by that marauding host was expected? It was a time of great confusion, the Danes avenging a huge massacre of their people by Ethelred the Unready a few years before. It seems likely that, if this illogical and inadequate dyke *does* date from the Saxons, it reflects the uncertainty and desperation of that stormy period.

I have an alternative theory, however. Supposing these stretches of ditch *do* date back to before the Saxons, and that we are mistaken in believing they are parts of a continuous whole. After all, what would the Saxons have been defending, if they were more concerned with farming the plain than with populating the hills? If earlier British people had wanted to clear large areas of the woodland, how would they have done it? By setting fire to it, of course. But there was no readily available water, and they would, in any case, have needed to protect their settlements and crops from the uncontrollable inferno of a forest fire during summer drought. The answer was to dig ditches. And what would be more natural than those early Christians, who probably knew the dyke's purpose perfectly well, naming the ditch not as having been *made* by the master of hell but as a barrier against him? Many traditional folk-tales associated with the Devil are associated with the ditch, and in a stretch at Hastoe, near Tring, you are supposed to be able to hear him rattling his chains, though this sounds like a confusion with some old ghost-story.

Talk of the Devil brings to mind another Chiltern curiosity.

Cymbeline's Mount. Cattle now guard the ancient hill-fort where the sons of the British king Cunobelin are reputed to have lost their lives defending their stronghold against the Romans.

Legend has it that if you run seven times round Cymbeline's Mount, near Wendover, you may raise the Devil up from hell. No doubt an hallucination brought on by total exhaustion, and, in any case, it is a tale attached to various hills and mounds throughout the country. The interesting thing about it is the mystical number seven.

There is more to Cymbeline's Mount than that, however. Its name comes from the popular belief that Cunobelin (Shakespeare's Cymbeline) was the tribal ruler of the Catuvellauni in these hills when the legions came at the bidding of Claudius to annex Britain to the Roman Empire. Shakespeare's version is memorable for one of his eternally repeatable phrases, but the living legend is that Cymbeline's sons were killed defending their stronghold on this hilltop.

"Pardon me, young man, but I am — what is the expression? — a little

rusty on minor Shakespeare. What is the memorable phrase to which you refer?"

"I have not slept one wink."

All one can say with certainty is that there are more questions than answers about Grim's Ditch and Cymbeline's Mount, and they remain what they have been for many hundreds of years – unsolved Chiltern mysteries, characteristically defiant of modern man's passion for facts.

What they have in common, however, and share with other and more modern aspects of Chilternism, is the survival of a powerful aura of paganism. Hills have a curious significance in the collective unconscious of the human race. Perhaps we feel more powerful, invulnerable or closer to the gods, when we rise above the common level. In countries where there are hills and mountains, the heights always have a strong hold on the minds of the people, and where there are none, the people build them for themselves – the pyramids of Egypt and Mexico, the church steeples of Europe, perhaps even the skyscrapers of New York. At any rate, the religious or psychological importance of altitude is especially marked around the prehistoric routes through the Chilterns.

It was mainly in their religious life that the Chilterns continued to assert their defiance of Authority, which was apt to regard both the hills themselves and the people living in them as 'wild and untamed', although the alternative view was sometimes heard that the people were merely rustic simpletons. Chiltern folk were implicated in the Lollard rising of 1413–14, and their loyalty to the Nonconformist cause lasted throughout the fifteenth century. They were steadfastly Puritan during the Civil War, and the Quakers in particular made many converts among them; right up to the nineteenth century the Chilterns formed a sort of frontier against the Church of England's stronghold on the south-east. One cannot help wondering if Bunyan saw the Chilterns as his Delectable Mountains.

The followers of Wycliffe's heresy may have been only a small minority of the lower-middle classes, but a few of them went to

Friends' Meeting House, Jordans. This famous Quaker meeting house was orig-
inally built in 1688 when the Toleration Act permitted Dissenters to build their
own places of worship. On the lawn are the graves of William Penn, his two
wives, Thomas Ellwood and other prominent Quakers.

the stake for their beliefs and established the Chilterns as a den of
heresy, with Lollard congregations at Amersham, Chesham and
High Wycombe, Marlow, Turville, Chinnor and elsewhere.
James Willis was the chief preacher of the lost Lollard cause after
the Oldcastle Rebellion. He was tried and condemned by the
Bishop of Lincoln at Wooburn and was soon followed to the stake
by his disciple William Aylward, of Henley-on-Thames, who
proclaimed that the Pope of Rome was "a great beast and a devil of
hell".

William Penn, although born in London and spending most of
his life there and in America, was a Chilterns man by ancestry and
temperament. He had much influence here, married Gulielma
Springett at Chorleywood and is buried outside the Friends' Meeting House at Jordans, near Chalfont St Peter. The son of Admiral
Sir William Penn, he was sent down from Oxford for being a Dis-

Penn church. The attractively mellow old church of Holy Trinity is famous for its association with the Penn family, and it contains memorials, including sculpture by Sir Francis Chantrey, to the Curzons, among which that to Assheton, Viscount Curzon, is the most notable.

senter, having adopted the religious principles of the founder of the Society of Friends, George Fox. Penn's father packed him off to Europe in a fury, but William continued his Quaker preaching when he returned and was frequently imprisoned. When his father died, he inherited a huge fortune and a claim on the Crown for £16,000, which was paid by a grant of land in America, where he founded Pennsylvania and its capital, Philadelphia, establishing there a colony for his persecuted Friends.

Penn's intimacy with James II enabled him to intercede on behalf of Quakers still in England, too, and although the charges of treasonable acts made against him by Macaulay have been much disputed, there can be little doubt that Penn's position at Court led him into political involvements which were certainly at odds with his professed faith. He was guilty of that hypocrisy that necessarily affects all pious Christians in modern society.

The poor and uneducated formed the bulk of the converts made in the Chilterns by the Quakers, who defended their emphasis on individual conscience against the "foule lyes and slanders" of Bunyan, whose influence spread southwards from Bedfordshire, and who had said that "Conscience is a poor dunghill creature in comparison of the Spirit." There was dissension as well as Dissent in the Chilterns, where Protestantism, in winning freedom from the tyranny of the Roman Church, also denied itself the comforts of confession and absolution and had to settle instead for the more drastic purgation of the psychiatrist. William Penn died in 1718 after a period of mental illness.

There is a grim realism and a grim irony in many Chiltern place-names. That misty imagining of a sublime rural tradition, so beloved of conservative topographers, which has been made to seem like paradise by the consequences of the Industrial Revolution, is really a mirage in the deserts of Chiltern. Settlement was possible only by winning a hard-fought battle against nature. It is a romantic fallacy to talk about a happy intercourse between man and nature in the Chilterns. It was actually a late surrender of nature to man after exhaustion from repeated rape; centuries of toil and sweat, turning forest into pasture for pigs and sheep; then digging chalk marl into the soil to turn it into fertile land. There is no romance in the blunt names of unproductive fields and bare bottoms that Chiltern settlers had to struggle with. (A bottom is a minor valley, I should hastily explain.) Villages with Ends and Bottoms are a common feature of the Chilterns and are often graphically described by their names: Pigtrough Bottom, Drunken Bottom, Hogspit Bottom. (On the other hand, the Chilterns have some of England's most charming village names, such as Britwell Salome, Christmas Common, Rotherfield Peppard, Parslow's Hillock and Chesham Bois – pronounced Chessum Boys.)

The farmers had enough problems on their plates without getting deeply involved in the religious disputes of the times. Most people simply got on with their own business. But then, they were reasonable men who adapted themselves to the world, and, as Shaw said, it is the unreasonable man who makes progress, by expecting the world to adapt itself to him. It was the Chiltern Puritans themselves, through their growing intolerance and taste for capitalism, who contributed a great deal to that destruction of the rural tradition which purists of today so much deplore. Irony may, in a sense, be regarded as the quintessence of Chilternism.

The Chilterns, anyway, won a reputation for swimming against the tide of English affairs and kept it up to and beyond the Industrial Revolution, when the railways exposed the area to the reach of better-off Londoners, who soon began that massive movement, still going on, of city workers to country residence, reversing the procedure which had continued through the previous four hundred years, ever since the Black Death: London's claws have torn the Chilterns' flesh, and the wounds do not heal.

For centuries the Chiltern inhabitants had earned their living from the land, as farmers and craftsmen, and the local economy rested to a large extent on the beechwoods. The Chilterns were practically the last refuge in England of some of the traditional woodland industries before mass-production made them extinct. If you walk through the graveyards of the Chiltern village churches, the bodies turning to dust beneath your feet will not, on the whole, be those of accountants, engineers, solicitors, secretaries and shop-assistants. They are the remains of farriers, wheelwrights, chair-bodgers, stonemasons, straw-plaiters, lace-makers and ploughmen, who plodded their particularly weary ways homeward on this discouraging soil.

By the time the Civil War ended, most of the woodland on the plains all round the Chilterns had been cleared for arable farming, but the hills themselves remained heavily wooded and provided much of London's fuel. Furniture-making gradually increased as the use of coal began to eliminate the need for logs, and the chair-making industry, especially, became concentrated in the Chiltern Hills. The manufacturers were centred in High Wycombe and a few other places, such as Stokenchurch and Penn, but the chair-bodgers were widely dispersed throughout the woods. They were

A Chiltern workshop. The big furniture-factories are concentrated in High Wycombe. This is the workshop of one of the smaller manufacturers, Aston Woodware, near Stokenchurch.

specialists in making the legs of chairs, supplying these to the men who made backs and seats and assembled the parts together. But the bodgers often made stools, tent-pegs and wheel-spokes as well.

The bodgers ('chairopodists' as they were apt to be called) were the most exclusive of the Chiltern craftsmen. They spent most of their lives in the woods, moving about like nomads and working in close communion with the beeches, calling spring and autumn "the bud and the brown". They were as important to the evolution of the woods as the trees were to their livelihood. Moving from plantation to plantation, they set up their primitive shacks and selected beeches for felling from the closely-grown trees of straight growth, being careful never to make large clearings but encouraging the upright growth of saplings by creating sufficient light and space. Thus fresh timber was always growing to replace that taken away. The bodger's main tools were saws, pole-lathe, axe and chisels, and a good man could turn eight hundred "cheer-legs" in a week. Legs "mead from split 'ood" were best, because those made from sound wood "ull breeak as soon as look at ye".

The men who made the complete chairs – Windsor and Chippendale, Sheraton and Hepplewhite patterns, but chiefly Windsor, for that was a Chiltern creation – gradually became factory-workers, and machinery made the legs. The sweet smell of shavings and sawdust left the woodland for the shop floor, until High Wycombe alone had over a hundred furniture factories, whose buyers selected their stocks of timber for the next few months' production from the falls in March and November.

The heels of women's shoes are usually made of beech – a fact that would not have sparked the slightest flicker of interest in a girl I saw at Coombe Hill, standing on high-heeled shoes quite unsuitable for the terrain, beside her boy-friend who was explaining the landscape spread out before them. If he thought he was giving her a treat, he was sadly mistaken – she was an unwilling witness of nature.

'The Hit or Miss', Penn Street. Standing opposite the village cricket pitch, the wisteria-clad old brick inn originally belonged to a chair-factory next door. It is virtually the pavilion for the local team, and a favourite rendezvous on summer evenings.

A century ago, she would have been supplementing the meagre income of her parents by straw-plaiting or lace-making. The Chilterns were always a relatively poor area, never enjoying the sort of prosperity that the wool trade brought to the Cotswolds in the Middle Ages. The lives of the people here were based on harsh realities. They could not hoist their television aerials above their cottage roofs and go sailing down their favourite channels into oceans of self-deception or complain to their shop stewards that the world was not treating them fairly. Their livelihoods were entirely in their own hands. If they were not capable of felling the trees, they could not make the chair-legs. They prized their independence of spirit as highly as their independence of means and had no intention of being moulded by kings or popes into citizens of standard format and orthodox character.

Straw-plaiting was the cottage industry of women and girls at the northern end of the Chilterns, generally speaking – Tring, Dunstable, Amersham and thereabouts – while lace-making was more common at the southern end. Said to have been introduced from France by Catherine of Aragon, the speciality here was bone-lace, or pillow-lace as it was called later. It was one of Buckinghamshire's most important industries for a long period. Local Members of Parliament won or lost votes according to their vehemence in denouncing the machine-made lace of Nottinghamshire, but of course it was the latter that won in the end.

Industry and commuterism have changed the face of the Chilterns – rather less than in many parts of the country, it is true, and mainly on the southern and eastern flanks – but the hills remain delightfully unspoiled in their more remote parts. The beechwoods are still among the glories of England. The spectacle of dazzling colour in a good autumn has to be seen to be believed, but even away from the woods the Chilterns seem to have their own distinctive colour. It is as if the chalk lends a fair complexion to the whole landscape, blending soft shades together with the restraint of a good artist's palette.

Oddly, artistic expression has not matched craftsmanship in the Chilterns. These landscapes are not such as attract painters, perhaps. They lack dramatic qualities, and their beauty comes not

Haymaking near Hazlemere. Though there is nothing peculiar to the Chilterns in this picture, it adds to the variety of the scene which some writers have rather blindly alleged to have a 'sameness' throughout the area.

from appearance only but depends on the combined sense of light and space and sound to make its emotional effect.

There is a considerable amount of common land in the hills, overgrown by scrub, where grazing rights are not used. In many cases, the rightful owners of land are not known, and though the soil is mostly poor, some of it is good land that was requisitioned for agricultural use during the war. The pattern of farming has been subject to constant change, swinging back and forth from predominantly arable to pasture land. A huge decline in all types of farming occurred towards the turn of the century, when the number of pigs and sheep kept in the hills was practically halved within fifty years. The world wars meant that some pasture was turned back to arable land, and nowadays a great variety of farming takes place in the hills.

There is also a great variety of animal, plant and bird life. Although the emphasis in the Chilterns is always on beech, there

Denizens of the Chiltern Hills. Well, what animals did you expect to find in the 'deserts of Chiltern'? (These are, in fact, Bactrian camels at Whipsnade Zoo.)

are fine oaks, the beautiful wild cherry and ash, holly, hornbeam, maple, juniper and many other trees. The area is famous among botanists, too, for its wild orchids, some of which are not found elsewhere.

The innumerable birds to be seen in the Chilterns have been catalogued by experts, but I can testify that, in addition to the long-tailed tits, treecreepers, jays, yellowhammers, warblers and whitethroats that are frequent visitors to my garden, as well as all the more obvious local residents, the collared dove, which has inhabited the area only since about 1960, sometimes seems almost as numerous as the sparrow.

The edible dormouse lives in the Chilterns, and the beechwoods are notable for the variety of snails to be found. Snails favour chalk country because they make their shells from the calcium. The red squirrel was common here at one time but has now been entirely replaced by the grey. There are plenty of foxes, hares and badgers, and among the larger mammals to be seen are rhino, tigers, bears, elephant . . . much the same as can be seen in many parts of Britain today, though the Chilterns may claim to have had them first.

The whole area is superb walking and riding country, with some fine views over the plain on the north-western side. In 1973 the Countryside Commission opened its Ridgeway long-distance footpath, which runs eighty-five miles from Ivinghoe Beacon to Overton Hill, near Marlborough, crossing the Thames at Goring. This follows, generally speaking, the ridge of the hills, but it is important to emphasize that it does not coincide with the Icknield Way, except for odd stretches here and there, since the four-thousand-year-old route is now surfaced road along much of its

Riding in the Chiltern beechwoods. Horse-riding is immensely popular throughout the Chilterns, with riding-schools and livery-stables everywhere. It is a curious fact that female riders outnumber males by three to one.

The Ridgeway Footpath at Coombe Hill. The monument is to the local dead in the South African War. It was rebuilt after being destroyed by lightning in 1938.

length, though in other parts it is still a deserted green lane.

When Lord Nugent of Guildford opened the footpath at Coombe Hill in 1973, the official party girded up its loins and dutifully set off on an inaugural walk along the long-distance path, setting us all a very fine example by covering the whole mile-and-a-half into the nearest town – Wendover.

Those with a more serious interest in walking will find the fifteen hundred miles of footpaths in the Chilterns splendid. They are well marked and are said to be the best-maintained in Britain. The chalk helps, by keeping the ground surface well drained, but the Chiltern Society can claim most of the credit for this distinction, having surveyed, signposted and cleared thousands of public rights of way and published an excellent series of maps of the area. It is only on foot that the Chiltern explorer can hope to penetrate some of the most ancient secrets of these hills.

Along with other destructions of rural life and tradition which the materialistic revolution brought in its wake, the belief in ghosts and witches was one. There are many ghost and witch stories in the Chilterns, though they appear to increase in number as one moves northwards. The nearer to Hertfordshire, perhaps, the more gullible the rustics, who were not, after all, nicknamed 'Hertfordshire Thickheads' for nothing. A small village, Great Gaddesden, had as many as three parishioners excommunicated at one point in the seventeenth century because they were believed bewitched.

The need for such escapist ideas is still with us, for we merely update them. Flying objects once identified as witches are now identified as beings from outer space. In the Chilterns, however, a loyalty to paganism lasted rather longer than elsewhere and is very much in line with the defiance of secular and ecclesiastical authority characteristic of the region. It is part of the stubborn independence which refused to be bombarded into that conformism for which the town-dwellers so easily fell.

The survival of paganism, which Christianity sought in vain to destroy and then perforce embraced, can be traced up to the present day: from medieval images, such as the mermaid suckling a lion in Edlesborough church, up to surviving country beliefs, the occasional appearances of Morris dancers, and so on. It reached its most bizarre and notorious climax, however – as far as the Chilterns are concerned – at West Wycombe in the eighteenth century, when Sir Francis Dashwood presided over what has come to be known as 'The Hell-Fire Club'.

It is a well-known Chiltern tale that always bears repeating, but it is important at the outset to note the distinction between paganism and Satanism. 'Hell-Fire Club' was a name given to the society by others, not by the members themselves, and there is no real evidence that Sir Francis and his friends ever practised black magic, whereas paganism is easily demonstrated and is clearly evident in nearly all Dashwood's works.

He was born in 1708 and received the customary classical education of the well-to-do, culminating in a series of Grand Tours.

Edlesborough church. Standing prominently on an artificial hill, in an overgrown church is worthy of greater care. Among other features,

churchyard and with a sign warning of falling masonry, this thirteenth-century it contains misericords of distinctly pagan influence.

West Wycombe House: the south front of the house, much modified by Lord le Despencer towards the end of the eighteenth century. The unusual double-deck colonnade, probably designed by John Donowell, has columns (Tuscan below, Corinthian above) of plastered timber. The church tower can be seen over the roof.

He lived at West Wycombe House, which had been the family home since 1698, and when he was twenty-four probably founded, or helped in founding, the Society of Dilettanti, which still exists. "The nominal qualification is having been in Italy," wrote Horace Walpole, "and the real one, having been drunk: the two chiefs are Lord Middlesex and Sir Francis Dashwood, who were seldom sober the whole time they were in Italy."

In 1741 Sir Francis was elected Tory MP for Romney, and he held the seat for the next twenty years. Meanwhile, in 1745 he married a wealthy widow, Sarah Ellis, and it was soon after this time that he founded his club in a London tavern, calling it at first 'the Brotherhood of Saint Francis of Wycombe'. The title indicates a rather juvenile taste for unconventional behaviour, as typical of the time as, say, smoking 'pot' is today. But during the following ten or fifteen years the club grew into something if not more sinister at any rate more improbable and eccentric.

One member of the society was Francis Duffield, who had bought a house converted from the ruined abbey at Medmenham. Before the Dissolution, the monks there had enjoyed a reputation for lawlessness. Duffield leased this house to Dashwood, who made it the headquarters of his club, where the members soon became known as 'the Monks of Medmenham'. Over the door was painted the motto "*Fay ce que voudras*" ("Do as you please"). A huge wine cellar was installed, well stocked with port and claret, and the members gathered for drinking and sexual adventures with the loose women they brought there and called their 'Nuns'.

The early members of the fraternity included Paul Whitehead, poet and journalist; the Earl of Sandwich, First Lord of the Admiralty; Thomas Potter, Paymaster-General and son of an Archbishop of Canterbury; John Wilkes, MP for Aylesbury and a later Lord Mayor of London; George Bubb Dodington, MP; Charles Churchill, a former clergyman turned poet, who built himself a neo-Gothic mansion at Chalfont St Peter; Henry Vansittart, Governor of Bengal; and the artist William Hogarth, who painted some of the other members, including Dashwood. Other alleged members included Frederick, Prince of Wales, the Earl of Bute, later Prime Minister, the Marquis of Granby, the Earl of March and Henry Fox, Lord Holland.

This aristocratic devotion to Bacchus and Venus would probably have gone down in the curiosities of eighteenth-century history as something either ludicrous or pathetic if political events had not made a sensation of it. Apart from Hogarth and Wilkes (who was in any case one of the first to leave it and instrumental in its downfall), the members were a gang of immature adventurers whose frolics would have provided as many case-histories for a psychiatrist as stories for the Press. One of the tarts who frequented Medmenham as a nun had a glass eye, and another was a well-known London 'madam'.

"That devil Wilkes", as George III called him, was undoubtedly the most interesting, if not the most admirable, member of the Brotherhood, and we have him to thank for some of our important constitutional rights. He had been educated at Leiden University and was an agnostic, but his fellow-members called him 'the Archbishop of Aylesbury'. He was a rabble-rouser of the first order, and a man of wit.

"Will you vote for me?" he asked his audience at an election meeting.

"I'd sooner vote for the Devil!" one of his hecklers shouted.

"But if your friend doesn't run," Wilkes retorted, "may I count on your support?"

The story goes that Wilkes once hid a baboon in the 'inner sanctum' at Medmenham and during a ceremony let it loose with horns fixed to its head. The gibbering ape leapt on the back of Lord Sandwich, who fell to his knees in terror, begging the Devil for mercy. The story is probably apocryphal, but that Sandwich became one of Wilkes's most bitter enemies is certain, and it would seem that some such unforgivable prank led to internal dissension in the club. Wilkes and Dashwood both had a taste for practical jokes. "You will either die from the pox, or be hanged," Sandwich is said to have told Wilkes, to which the latter replied: "That depends whether I embrace your principles or your mistress."

In 1761 Sir Francis Dashwood was elected MP for Weymouth, and in the following year Lord Bute appointed him Chancellor of the Exchequer – an unconscious practical joke at the expense of the nation, for Dashwood had a "profound aversion to mathematics". Wilkes and Charles Churchill, arch-rivals of the government's principles, now started to let the cat out of the bag regarding the Medmenham frolics, and, according to legend, Dashwood toned down the club's activities and moved his HQ to the caves he had excavated below West Wycombe Hill. During all this time, he had been busy with alterations to the house and grounds of West Wycombe Park, where he had accumulated a large library of pornography and much indecent statuary and was rebuilding St Lawrence's Church with the golden globe on top. This was

The church of St Lawrence, West Wycombe, rebuilt and refurnished by Sir Francis Dashwood. The gold leaf for the gilded globe, in which drinking parties were held, is said to have come from the Venice Customs building.

reached by an iron ladder with chain handrails, leading to a trap-
door, and inside were three seats where members could retreat for
a cramped drinking-party – "the best Globe Tavern I was ever
in", Wilkes quipped.

Dashwood's first budget was greeted with incredulous derision
in the House of Commons, and Lord Bute's appalling government
was not long in falling, but Dashwood was an able man and not
yet notorious, for in 1763 a lapsed family barony was restored in
his favour and he became Lord le Despencer, and Lord Lieutenant
of Buckinghamshire. Then Pitt appointed him Postmaster General, an office in which he showed great aptitude for adminis-
tration. He became friendly during this period with his American
counterpart, Benjamin Franklin, who spent some time in England.
Together they produced a revised Book of Common Prayer
which is still in use in the United States, though it was ignored in
England. This work cannot be interpreted as a late return to ortho-
doxy on Dashwood's part. He seems to have remained an unre-
lenting paradox to the end of his life, happily mixing a pagan
philosophy with a strong sense of Christian duty.

Naturally, gossip has linked Franklin's name with 'the Hell-Fire
Club', but it is not certain that he was ever a member of it. If the
club was not already defunct by this time, it certainly cannot have
been very active. Its surviving members were old men, Dashwood
himself being sixty-five. His wife had died in 1769, and he lived at
West Wycombe with a former actress, Mrs Barry. Duffield,
Dodington, Potter, Churchill and Hogarth were in their graves,
and Whitehead, who had already been middle-aged when he "settled down to a life of debauchery", died in 1774. His heart was
placed in an urn in Dashwood's newly-built pagan mausoleum
beside the church. Dried and shrunken, the ghastly organ was
shown to visitors for years afterwards, until some collector of
macabre relics stole it. Dashwood himself died in 1781, aged
seventy-three.

Truth and fiction are impossible to separate with certainty from
the legend of 'the Hell-Fire Club' which has grown up over two
centuries. The fact that it is still called by a name its members never
gave it is sufficient proof of the determination of scandal-mongers

to make the most of the opportunities for juicy stories. Rumours of satanic orgies, obscene rites, black magic, secret passages, unspeakable paintings, drinking wine from human skulls, entrances in the shape of vaginas, and many other examples which are either unbelievably depraved or excruciatingly funny, according to your point of view, are still circulated, but it is well known that many of them were invented by political enemies of Sir Francis and by later embroiderers of the tale, including Byron. On the other hand, it has to be admitted that there are strong suggestions of demonism in Hogarth's portrait of Sir Francis in his monk's robes, and not *all* the stories about the club can have been invented.

Sir Francis Dashwood's successors (he left no legitimate heirs) lost no time in calling in experts to refashion West Wycombe Park. Humphrey Repton re-designed the gardens and was evidently instructed to remove the more questionable imagery. Much of the splendid decoration remains inside the house, which is now National Trust property. It is curious that pre-Christian actions are called 'pagan', but pre-Christian paintings are called 'classical'. West Wycombe House is sufficient evidence of Lord le Despencer's classical tastes, but just how far his paganism went is another of those secrets the Chilterns prefer to keep hidden.

There are more recent secrets associated with the other great Chiltern house, Cliveden, which was leased at one period to Frederick, Prince of Wales (who died there) and visited by Lord Bute. The long arm of coincidence reaches across Chiltern unorthodoxy.

Viscount Astor's close friends in the late 1950s included an osteopath named Stephen Ward, who rented a cottage on the estate and who numbered people of very high standing among his patients and people of very low morals among his friends. How far the two categories overlapped is still among the secrets, but in 1961, while the Astors were entertaining the Minister for War and his wife in the big house, Ward was entertaining, or being entertained by, a Russian diplomat and a prostitute in the little one. The outcome of this was a brief affair between the Minister, Mr John Profumo, and the prostitute, Miss Christine Keeler, which Profumo broke off when the Foreign Office got wind of it and warned him that he

The Fountain of Love, Cliveden. Designed and made by the sculptor Ralph Waldo Story, the fountain replaced a statue of a previous owner, the Duke of Sutherland, which Viscount Astor, God bless him, shifted to a more hidden site.

was swimming in dangerous waters.

Unfortunately for Mr Profumo, an ex-boy-friend of Christine Keeler's, a West Indian named Edgecombe, attacked her with a gun whilst she was visiting her friend Mandy Rice-Davies, a teen-aged tart who had recently been the mistress of a slum-property racketeer, Peter Rachman. This incident brought the matter into court, where the defendant Edgecombe, who got seven years, was just about the last person of any interest to the Press, which sniffed a major scandal and helped to provoke it. Questions asked in the House of Commons were answered dishonestly by Mr Profumo, who subsequently resigned from a career which had been thought to hold great promise for the nation.

The Establishment, thoroughly ruffled, sought a scapegoat for its embarrassment and fixed on Stephen Ward, who was arrested in Watford and brought to trial for living on immoral earnings and on other charges. Confident that his society friends would protect him, Ward was soon disillusioned. Terrified of exposure, the public men involved became rooted to their spots like mesmerized rabbits. To a man they deserted Ward in his hour of greatest need, and before the inevitable 'guilty' verdict was brought in, he took an overdose of sleeping pills and died three days later.

This whole miserable shambles of British justice has special relevance to the Chilterns, not only because the particular affair began here but also because the Chilterns have to some extent fostered the hypocrisy that allowed Ward's sacrifice. The English are naturally conservative but not naturally puritanical. Puritanism is, and always was, a mask hiding the real human being behind it. The spectacle of the English in "one of their periodical fits of morality" may have struck Macaulay as ridiculous, but at times it is too disgusting and offensive to laugh at. We sit in church or in front of our newspapers – a vast congregation of malingerers, adulterers, liars, shop-lifters, tax-evaders, child-beaters, traffic-offenders, expense-account fiddlers, gamblers and drunkards – and throw up our hands in horror whenever a public figure is exposed for behaving with anything less than Christ-like virtue. We used to send men to their deaths from ignorance. Now we do so from malice. Ask the present-day mob who will cast the first stone, and the volunteers will step forward.

As we set out to look round the Chiltern Hills in more detail in the following chapters, we shall come across instances of martyrdom and heroism that led specifically to some of the freedoms we cherish, but if we are led into thinking of them as struggles against medieval intolerance and oppression, we should remember Stephen Ward. We are still capable today of making a martyr of a Chiltern heretic.

CHAPTER 2

THE TAIL-END:
HERTFORDSHIRE
AND BEDFORDSHIRE

THE TOWN CENTRE of Dunstable is not, it must be admitted, the most promising place from which to start an exploration of Chiltern country. Not all the legionaries of Roman Britain, with their martial tread and clanking armour, could have created a more alarming prospect of chaos and danger in Durocobrivae than is now a daily routine at the traffic-infested crossing of Watling Street and the Icknield Way.

Yet it is no more than a few minutes' walk from here to the Five Knolls barrows and the Downs, where, despite the motor-cars that pack the area in summer to watch the activities of the London Gliding Club, the first hints of Chiltern landscape can be found. The chalk escarpment rises steeply from the vale and exposes its pale breast, with the Whipsnade Lion tattooed large upon it, to wind, rain and setting sun.

It is a somewhat raucous overture to a concert of tasteful restraint, and it is not easy, here, to dismiss the effects of civilization and see the prospect before us with the eyes of palaeolithic man. Nor does the collection of the London Zoological Society help us much in this respect, for even if our imagination is able to transform

Dunstable Downs. The view from the northern extremity of the sightseer's Chilterns, looking across southern Bedfordshire, with the London Gliding Club's property in the foreground.

Whipsnade Park Zoo. The Indian elephant is one of the first animals to greet visitors to the famous Chiltern grounds of the London Zoological Society. As well as the great variety of animals and birds, there are some fine views from the western edge of the park.

the captives brought from India and Canada into sabre-toothed tigers and hunting wolves, the presence of hippopotamuses on this English chalk hill, and penguins in this waterless region, tends to destroy the illusion.

The Society bought over four hundred acres of the Ashridge estate in Bedfordshire, when it was sold in the twenties, for the zoo which was opened in 1931 and named Whipsnade after the village spread about a large common nearby. It was the first zoo of its kind, where the animals were allowed some small degree of freedom, and of course it remains by far the most popular of Chiltern attractions – indeed, one of the very few places in the Chilterns, mercifully, where parking-space for coaches is a necessity.

My own opinion is that the zoo is best visited in winter, when it is much quieter, and some of the animals, such as the Canadian timber wolves, the polar bears, reindeer and penguins, seem more at home than during an English summer. Some animals and birds, on the other hand, have to be given special protection during an icy winter. The beautiful rosy flamingoes, for example, would stand in the water while it froze over and then break their legs trying to get out. Sea lions would drown beneath solid ice, and the skins of elephants have to be rubbed with vegetable oil to prevent cracking in extremes of temperature to which they are not naturally accustomed. The gibbons have to be taken off their island to prevent their escape. They are confined only by the surrounding moat which they will not enter, but if it froze over, they would cross quite happily. The eerie sound of wolves howling at night is a familiar one to me, since I lived within barking distance of Whipsnade for some years.

Kensworth and Studham are Whipsnade's neighbouring villages in Bedfordshire, Studham being the highest village in that county. Both were in Hertfordshire until 1897, and Hertfordshire, a conservative county if ever there was one, may have been quietly glad to get rid of them. They had been troublesome in both secular and ecclesiastical matters. Bunyan's influence was particularly strong there, and one of the first Baptist congregations was formed at Kensworth. This may explain why both villages moved away from the parish churches at their original centres. Or possibly, in the case of Kensworth, it was because of the headless ghost of a milkmaid that haunted a lane near the church.

Later, when a large number of the women in these poor villages were involved in straw-plaiting to supplement the pittance earned by the menfolk, they had good cause to feel threatened when the government began to promote the sale of felt hats in order to help the wool trade. The local villages delivered a petition pointing out that over a thousand families depended on the straw-plait trade for their livelihood. Ironically, it was the war with France that restored the villagers' security, by putting a temporary halt to the competition from Italian straw hats.

While the lace-makers of Buckinghamshire were growing short-sighted and deformed with their work, the straw-plaiters of Bedfordshire and Hertfordshire were causing much concern to social-workers. "A large average of the women," gasped one easily-shocked rector, "have illegitimate children, and some at such an early age as quite to startle even those who are at home in criminal statistics." Well, the 'wild and untamed' Chilterns were behaving true to form, that is all.

Ivinghoe Beacon. The terminus of the Ridgeway footpath, this ancient hill-fort is also the point at which the Icknield Way divides into its Upper and Lower courses. 756 feet above sea level, its peak commands fine views in all directions.

It is convenient at this point to cross over into a tongue of Buckinghamshire before dealing with the Hertfordshire Chilterns, because Beacon Hill, or Ivinghoe Beacon as it is known locally, is not only the highest point at this end of our exploration; it is also the point where the Icknield Way splits into its Upper and Lower courses, and where the Ridgeway footpath reaches its terminus.

The hill was an Iron Age hill-fort, surrounded by a triangular ditch, and there are burial mounds nearby. The views from the top are magnificent in every direction and include the church at Edlesborough, perched on a hill which was clearly made by man and not by nature. One of the misericords in the choir has a splendidly pagan carving of a lion drinking from a mermaid's breast.

The Ivinghoe Hills, leading southwards from here towards Ashridge, are owned by the National Trust, and the B489 road which skirts the northern foot of Beacon Hill is the Icknield Way, arriving at a T-junction that no Celtic traveller ever dreamed of, leading to Ivinghoe village in one direction and to Pitstone in the other. From the junction one can see a restored post-mill which has the date 1627 carved on one of its timber beams. It is generally assumed that this is the date of the mill's construction, though it

Pitstone Mill. Dated 1627 on one of its timbers, this is probably England's oldest surviving post-mill. It was once owned by the Grand Junction Canal Company. Wrecked by a storm, it has been restored by the National Trust. In the background, the Pitstone cement works.

could have been built earlier, of course. It is certainly one of the oldest surviving windmills in England. It was standing in this field when Charles I had just ascended the throne of England, before Rembrandt had become famous in the Netherlands, before Shah Jehan had built the Taj Mahal in Agra.

The view of the mill is rather ruined from the approach side by the presence of the huge Pitstone cement-works behind it, but we should not be too quick to condemn this eyesore of modern industry, for the tradition of mining and quarrying in this vicinity goes back a very long way. There is an ancient flint mine here, and chalk quarrying was begun by the Romans, for they, too, needed cement for their buildings.

Ivinghoe is an attractive village with a surprisingly large and stately church, inside which is an hour-glass, affixed to the pulpit, for which many a congregation has no doubt been truly thankful. Ivinghoe once had an administrative importance one would hardly suspect today, if it were not hinted at by the size of its church, and it also has a building that was once its Town Hall.

The so-called Tring Gap breaks the high ground along the borders of Buckinghamshire and Hertfordshire, and this is a place of engineering feats. In this case, also, we ought to be cautious in deploring the imposition of modern industry on the Chiltern landscape, for just south of Tring, via Wigginton Bottom, passes one of the stretches of Grim's Ditch, and the Romans, too, took their military road through the gap itself. Large-scale engineering works are a commonplace here.

The Grand Union Canal (originally the Grand Junction Canal) was the first of the modern transport developments. Part of a plan to link the Trent with the Thames, so that coal and other freight could be conveyed more economically from the Midlands to London, it was engineered by William Jessop and had reached Tring by the end of the eighteenth century. Jessop had foreseen

The Grand Union Canal near Marsworth. A long series of locks raises the canal to nearly four hundred feet to take it through the Chilterns via the Tring Gap. It is the highest artificial watercourse in England, and the only water to penetrate the Chiltern escarpment.

that taking the canal through the Chilterns would be his biggest problem, and near Marsworth the watercourse is raised by a long series of locks to nearly four hundred feet above sea level. Not only is it the highest artificial watercourse in England, but it is the only water to penetrate the Chiltern escarpment. Its height meant that reservoirs had to be constructed from which water could be pumped to the canal, and these are now nature reserves where a great variety of bird life can be seen.

In October 1902, during a serious drought, the *Daily Mail* reported: "Heroic exertions on the part of the Grand Junction Company's engineer and servants do not enable more than eighty or ninety barges a week to pass over the Tring Summit, whereas in times of plentiful water 130 pass. . . . An extraordinary meeting of boatmen stretches three miles along the bank and never adjourns. Their horses lie down and go to sleep, their wives sit knitting and gossip, their children playing in the fields. . . ."

Those were the days! But they were already numbered, the London and Birmingham Railway having brought another engineering wonder, ominous to canal shareholders, to the Tring Gap. The long and deep railway-cutting stretching northwards from Tring Station was reckoned to be one of the feats of the age. Men and horses moved one and a half million tons of earth from this stretch, but I suppose it is exceedingly rare for an Inter-City traveller from Euston to reflect on the loss of life and limb that contributed to his fast and comfortable journey today. A far cry from the days when Tring people used to walk to Aston Hill a couple of miles away, to see an epitaph cut into the turf to a shepherd named Faithful, who had been buried on the hill which was his favourite spot.

Tring itself is of doubtful interest to the Chiltern explorer, and the motorist can conveniently by-pass the town on the latest development, a motorway loop off the A41, which bisects Tring Park, where Wren designed a house for Sir Henry Guy. This mansion was subsequently bought by Baron Lionel de Rothschild, who rebuilt it, and the second baron stocked the park with all manner of birds and animals, including zebras, which he used to draw his carriage to town; he founded the Tring Museum, which is now part of the British Museum's Natural History section.

Wigginton was long ago nicknamed 'Wicked Wigginton' because it was notoriously undisciplined. Its publicans were alleged never to turn a customer away, regardless of licensing hours, and cockfights were arranged there long after the sport had been banned.

Gubblecote, near Marsworth, was even more notorious. In 1751 an old couple, John and Ruth Osborn, were murdered by a mob which had been persuaded that they were witches. Sixteen years after the death penalty for witchcraft had been abolished, a local rabble, led by a chimney-sweep named Thomas Colley, dragged the couple out of the church to which they had fled in terror, stripped them naked and dragged them, tied together, through a pond. Ruth Osborn was drowned, and her husband died soon afterwards. Colley was hanged for the crime, and his body hung in chains on a gibbet.

The Ridgeway footpath near Tring passes the grounds of Pendley Manor, now an adult education centre but for centuries the home of the Williams family, lords of the manor, whose present representative is the well-known horseman and broadcaster Dorian Williams.

The reader may be relieved to learn that, having passed the barrier of the Tring Gap, we can entirely forget industry for a while and concentrate on more 'rural' Chiltern country. Where better to start than the unspoiled Hertfordshire village of Aldbury, a little to the east? It lies below the escarpment rising to the first true Chiltern beauty-spot and is itself one of the most photographed villages in all the Chilterns.

The large village horse-pond, surrounded by brick-and-timber cottages and the former village bakehouse, is marred only by the presence of stocks and whipping-post, which with typical native hypocrisy have now come to be regarded as quaint attractions on village greens throughout England. But the stocks gave their name to a house just outside the village, as well as to the road it stands near, where literature has been well served.

'Stocks', set back from the road behind a farmhouse, became the home of Mrs Humphry Ward, the Victorian novelist and one of

Aldbury. The most attractive and unspoiled village in the Hertfordshire Chilterns, it nestles below the beech-clad escarpment rising to the Ashridge estate. The central building with tall chimney was once the village bakehouse.

'Goliath'. An uprooted and mutilated beech near Aldbury, showing the typical spreading and shallow root system. A dead tree like this will support a multitude of insect life as well as fungi.

the first women magistrates. Mrs Ward was the niece of Matthew Arnold, mother-in-law of the historian G.M. Trevelyan and aunt to Aldous and Julian Huxley, who both spent many happy days in this house. Other writers came here, too, such as Henry James and Bernard Shaw (who hardly saw eye to eye with his hostess's curiously unprogressive views on women's suffrage).

Squire Harcourt of this village, who died in the eighteenth century and has a monument in the church, is said to haunt the road towards Tring, driving along it in a coach drawn by phantom horses whose hooves and jangling harness are sometimes heard.

In the hills above Aldbury is one of the most spectacular of Chiltern places, which no visitor to the area should miss. Yet I have been astonished to find how many people in central Hertfordshire have never *heard* of Ashridge, much less seen it. The story is that Richard, Earl of Cornwall, Henry III's brother, brought back from one of his crusades a golden box containing what was said to be blood from the body of Christ. And lest any heretic, Chiltern or otherwise, should doubt the authenticity of this coagulated souvenir, its genuineness had been acknowledged by the Patriarch of Jerusalem, no less, who was soon to become Pope Urban IV. In 1276 Richard's son Edmund founded a monastery here at Ashridge

*Ashridge House. Built by James Wyatt on the site of a monastery, and surrounded
training college. It contains*

by fine beechwoods, the former home of the Egerton family is now a management a spectacular hall and chapel.

where the box could be kept, and for 250 years the monks lived among the Chiltern beechwoods, receiving the simple devotion of paupers and the rich endowments of princes who came in pilgrimage (to say nothing of other favours, if we believe the old story that a secret passage connected the monastery with a nearby nunnery!).

Then Henry VIII suppressed the monastery and exposed the relic as a fake, taking over the building as a home for his three children. Elizabeth was staying here when she was arrested on suspicion of being involved in the plot to remove Bloody Mary from the throne. After Elizabeth's death, her Lord Keeper of the Seal, Sir Thomas Egerton, bought Ashridge, and the Egerton family owned it for the next three centuries, becoming dukes of Bridgewater in the process.

It is the third Duke, Francis, whose story dominates Ashridge during the Egerton period and whose tall monument stands there today, though ironically he spent little time there and allowed the place to fall into ruin. He inherited the title at the age of twelve and grew to be a man of enormous body and little mind. He was undoubtedly a little mad. He swore he would never again speak to a woman after his fiancée broke off their engagement, and as far as we know he kept his word, never even allowing a female servant into the house. He once starved a horse to death because it had thrown him, and threatened to shoot anyone who gave it food or drink. His fame, however, rests on a piece of inspiration which earned him the title 'Father of Inland Navigation'. He teamed up with the illiterate engineering genius James Brindley, one supplying the cash and the other the know-how, and off they went – Butch Egerton and the Some Dunce Kid – and built the first entirely artificial canal in Britain, to carry coal from the Duke's mines at Worsley into Manchester. It cut the price of coal in the city by almost half.

It was left to the seventh Earl of Bridgewater to rebuild Ashridge, and he employed James Wyatt, that specialist in the sham-Tudor style of architecture, who had been nicknamed 'The Destroyer' after his drastic restorations of various cathedrals. Wyatt built the present mass of pinnacles, towers and pointed windows before dying of shock after his coach overturned (poetic jus-

The Bridgewater Monument, Ashridge. The fluted Doric column to 'the Canal Duke' was erected in 1832. It is 108 feet high, and has 172 steps, which may be climbed, by those with sufficient stamina, for a view of the surrounding country.

tice, some might say, since he had caused a great deal of shock to purists in his time). The house has been called a "wedding cake" by Massingham, and "spectacular" by Pevsner, but whatever one thinks of it, the place is unquestionably one of the most striking expressions of the Gothic Revival. (The spire on the chapel is a fibreglass replacement, lowered into position by helicopter in 1969!) Ashridge House is now a management college for industry.

The huge park surrounding the house is National Trust property, and here the Chiltern beeches are seen at their finest – surprisingly, perhaps, since this north-eastern end of the hills is generally much more open than the parts nearer the Thames. A herd of fallow deer and a few muntjac roam here, though one is lucky to catch sight of them. In summer the road leading from Berkhamsted, heavily infested with cars, might be off-putting to the country-lover, but one can easily escape by walking a few yards away from the conglomeration. The woods are a source of constant delight, with splendid views towards Aylesbury from the western edge, overlooking Aldbury, and in autumn they offer spectacles of saffron and scarlet, green and gold, cinnamon and crimson.

Berkhamsted Common, over a thousand acres adjoining the Ashridge estate, is one of the largest commons in southern England, and in 1865 it became the subject of a long and important legal battle when Lord Brownlow, then owner of Ashridge, tried to enclose some of it to form a deer park, putting five-feet-high fences around it. A local landowner who had not sold his rights of commonage transported a gang of navvies up from London, pulled down the fences during the night and took Lord Brownlow to court. The case dragged on for four years but finally resulted in the preservation of the ancient rights, by one of which the poor of Berkhamsted had been permitted in medieval times to gather the wood of the gorse bushes for fuel.

Berkhamsted is geographically entitled to be called a Chiltern town, but the birthplace of the poet William Cowper and the storyteller Graham Greene has little to recommend it visually to the attention of Chiltern explorers. It sits, pulverized, modernized and commuterized, astride the frantic A41 of Roman origin, and its castle, associated with Becket and Chaucer, Piers Gaveston and the Black Prince, is an unpicturesque and barely existent ruin.

The memorials to the earls and dukes of Bridgewater, and other members of the Egerton family, are contained in the church at Little Gaddesden, and from the corner of the churchyard there is a view towards Studham worth pausing over. This village was reputedly the home of John of Gaddesden, Edward III's physician, who makes a brief appearance in *The Canterbury Tales*. It was certainly the home of Rosina Massey, one of Hertfordshire's

Sculpture at Little Gaddesden. This Raphaelesque relief is part of a monument to John William Egerton, seventh Earl of Bridgewater, who rebuilt Ashridge. It is in the village church and is one of the masterpieces of Sir Richard Westmacott, whose work can also be seen in Ashridge House.

Kings Langley. Sloping down to the valley of the River Gade, this road joins the Roman Akeman Street, now the A41.

best-known witches, and it was towards Studham that she was sometimes seen flying (or if not her, at least her three-legged stool, which ran errands for her). And it was the home of William Ellis, one of the earliest popular agricultural writers.

Nowadays, it is difficult to separate the witch from the doctor. John of Gaddesden's book of charms and cures was considered a collection of 'old fables' by many. Nor was Ellis any improvement. He reported the cure of a girl with the "Evil in her feet" by the device of cutting off a hind leg and foreleg of a toad, tying them in a silk bag and hanging it round the girl's neck.

The Hertfordshire Chilterns continue down the county's western edge with a group of villages around Kings Langley and end at Chorleywood, which spills over the border into Buckinghamshire. Kings Langley (so named because Henry III built a palace there which was occupied at various times by all the Plantagenet monarchs) slopes down from its green to the valley of the Gade, where the modern road and the railway cut through it on their way to the Tring Gap. The village originated higher up the hillside but gradually moved towards the Roman road to take advantage of passing trade.

It was originally called Chiltern Langley, and there is a record of a carpenter being employed to make traps in the thirteenth century in an effort to protect livestock from the marauding wolves that still roamed the area in those days. Later, an Aldbury man staying at 'The Saracen's Head' there was robbed of five gold coins, probably by the landlord. This inn can trace its history back to the sixteenth century, standing in what was then known as 'Dronken Lane'.

Bovingdon nestles in the motherly bosom of two hills – a straggling village, but a true Chiltern one when we recall that two of its sons were executed for their involvement in the Oldcastle Rebellion. Ask the older natives to direct you to Bovingdon Docks. The Chiltern taste for irony is present here, too.

Flaunden is another village which moved its centre of population some distance from its point of origin. The ruined former village church could still be seen, early in this century, crumbling in a spinney beside the Chess near Latimer, but not a stone of it now remains, each one, no doubt, helping to form an old wall in the vicinity.

Some cottages were built against the wall of the church at one time, and a woman living in one of them told a visitor she hoped it would rain on Sunday so that the parson would not come. She had a hen sitting on thirteen eggs in the pulpit! Corpses sometimes lay in isolated village churches for days awaiting burial, when bad weather kept the parsons away.

The Two Brewers Inn at Chipperfield, in which prize-fighters were once trained, looks out on the village common, together with the church and manor house, all forming an attractive setting for summer cricket, far removed from the atmosphere centuries ago when the women of the village got into trouble for jeering at Richard III as he rode here during a stay at Langley Palace. The

King took his revenge by decreeing that henceforth the widows of the parish should not be permitted the dowries from their husband's estates when the men died intestate.

The best of modern jeers is reserved for a house not far from here which was the subject of one of H.J. Massingham's most splendid insults:

> We counted ten gables of different shapes along the front, eight oriels, also variegated, and forty-five windows, all latticed if I remember aright. There was still plenty of room for what seemed an acre of brickwork in different shades, a labyrinth of half-timbering, heavily pargetted plasterwork, yards and yards of highly-ornamented barge-boarding, mansarded roof-gables and an elevated wood of the tudorest of Tudor chimneys. It looked like seven Moreton Old Halls, as reconstructed at Hollywood, transhipped in segments, touched up in the Tottenham Court Road and then set in a row on Commonwood Common.

Pevsner evidently felt that the best way of dealing with this building was to ignore it altogether. One end of the house has been burned down in recent years, however, so it is no longer quite so hideous as in Massingham's day, if only because there is not so much of it, and, after a variety of uses since the war, it has now been divided into flats.

Length is the main feature of the village green at Sarratt which, like Flaunden, has moved away from its original centre. When Sir Henry Chauncy wrote his *Historical Antiquities of Hertfordshire* in 1700, he declared that Sarratt's church was at the centre of the village, but it is certainly not now. The church has a saddle-back roof, unique in Hertfordshire. Sarratt is of Roman origin, and there is an early homestead site in the woods near Rosehall Green, but the modern village is a curious hotch-potch of architectural styles that give it the appearance of a fruit salad when compared with a real peach of a village such as Aldbury.

The village was nicknamed 'Backward Sarratt', even by the slow-moving populace known as 'Hertfordshire Hedgehogs', but

Commonwood Common House. Part of this extraordinary house, near Sarratt, has been burned down since Massingham likened it to a Hollywood version of a Tudor mansion.

The River Chess near Sarratt. This pleasant little river gives Chesham its name and is seen here flowing past Sarratt Mill House, where a paper-mill once stood.

View near Sarratt. Although the most spectacular views are obtained from the Chilterns is typical of the rolling

...estern flanks of the hills and in the southern parts, this scene in the Hertfordshire ...untryside throughout the area.

it was not too backward to be true to Chiltern form, for a curate named Thomas Hemingforth was expelled from the living here in 1485 for 'apostasy'. He was obviously one of the Chiltern Lollards.

All this north-eastern part of the Chilterns was famous at one time for its cherry orchards, where the sweet and fleshy fruit known as 'Hertfordshire Black' was grown in abundance. The wild cherry is common in the woods all around and is one of the most beautiful of Chiltern trees, its pale blossom falling like snow-flakes when the wind gets in its branches, and then in early autumn turning to brilliant splashes of scarlet and orange before the fall. 'Cherry-pickers' was a popular nickname for the natives in these west Hertfordshire villages, and the word 'cherry' is still to be found everywhere in the names of farms, fields, streets and houses.

Buried in the churchyard at Chorleywood is Sir George Alexander, the famous, handsome and shrewd actor-manager who ran the St James's Theatre in London for the quarter of a century before his death. He urged Oscar Wilde into writing much of his finest work and put on the first productions of some of it, frequently giving Wilde money in advance for work he took ages to deliver. (When he offered Wilde a thousand pounds for his rights in *Lady Windermere's Fan*, the author replied: "I have such excellent confidence in your judgement, my dear Alec, I have no alternative but to refuse.") Most of Wilde's characters are named after places in England, and his Chiltern people are Lord Goring, the Earl of Caversham and Sir Robert Chiltern. It seems rather remiss of him, in the circumstances, not to have named one of them the Hon Mrs Chorley-Wood. After Wilde's conviction, Alexander fell into the hypocritical mood of the time and removed the author's name from the posters and programmes while continuing to make money from the production, but he later realized the importance of being honest and made amends by regular payments to Wilde for the plays he had acquired very cheaply through the author's bankruptcy.

Chorleywood – so called, according to a story so absurd that it is probably true, because the Merry Monarch or his old man once rested in the wood there: hence 'Charley Wood' – is a high-class residential village built around its large common, and it leads us

Chorleywood Common. Among the largest of the Chiltern commons, it has the usual golf course, much gorse and some nice views over the Chess valley.

over the county border into Buckinghamshire, leaving behind the Chilterns of Hertfordshire where, in spite of the attractions of places such as Ashridge and Aldbury, we have not yet encountered what might be called typical Chiltern country.

Hertfordshire is predominantly arable farming land, famous for its wheat and barley, whereas the more characteristic Chiltern scene is one of mixed farming, where the crops are intermingled with grazing sheep and cattle on the hillside pasture-land. All the Hertfordshire area is also commuter territory, very much over-populated and over-developed.

Let us therefore persevere into Buckinghamshire, where there are untold delights in store for us. "The farther you go," as Tintoretto said, "the deeper is the sea."

"And what, pray, has Tintoretto to do with the Chilterns?"

"Nothing whatever, madam, but come with me and we shall glimpse treasures as unexpected in the deserts of Chiltern as if we had suddenly turned up in Venice."

Chiltern harvest. The word 'harvest' comes from the Anglo-Saxon 'haerfest', barley being especially common, and these roly-poly bales

84

meaning autumn. A variety of cereal crops is grown on the Chiltern arable land,
are a picturesque result of modern agricultural machinery.

Chenies Manor House. The remains of a much larger early-Tudor mansion, the home of the Russell family, earls of Bedford, until they made Woburn their chief seat. Note the superbly ornamented chimneys.

CHAPTER 3

THE HEART:
BUCKINGHAMSHIRE

THE FIRST STOP in Buckinghamshire after crossing over into the
county from Chorleywood is Chenies, a neat 'model' village
arranged round a green where, set back beyond the church, are the
surviving wings of a Tudor manor house. This must have been a
huge mansion in the sixteenth century, for it became the home of
the Russells, dukes of Bedford, and remained so until, moving to
Woburn, they allowed Chenies to fall into neglect. Now its
remaining mellow brickwork, gables, elaborately twisted chimneys and transomed windows give a glimpse of what a great house
it must have been when Queen Elizabeth and her retinue were
entertained here.

However, it is the nearby church that is a treasure-house unique
not only in the Chilterns but in the whole of England. As you enter
the small, dark church, it appears unexceptional, but right along
the north side of the nave and chancel, separated from them by a
screen of wood and glass, is the Bedford Chapel, where the dukes
and others of the Russell family lie. This private family chapel is
not open to the public, but by pressing one's face against the glass
one can, like a child looking in the window of a sweet-shop,
glimpse the sumptuous contents that Pevsner has called "the richest
single storehouse of funeral monuments in any parish church of
England". Among the earls and countesses, dukes and duchesses is

the memorial to Lord John Russell, the Prime Minister, the first of many Prime Ministers we shall come across in the Buckinghamshire Chilterns. Berkshire might be the royal county, but Buckinghamshire, across the river, is where the power lies.

The neighbouring village is Latimer, where the green sports a more modest, if queerer, memorial – to a horse which was involved in saving the life of a lord of the manor, Lord Chesham, during the Boer War. Latimer House, Lord Chesham's former home, stands prominently on the hillside and looks inviting from below, but it is now the Ministry of Defence's Joint Services Staff College.

Following the course of the River Chess upstream, we come naturally enough to Chesham, one of the larger Chiltern towns but a curiously disappointing one today, transformed from the place that William Cobbett, a century and a half ago, called "a nice little town, lying in a deep and narrow valley, with a stream of water running through it". And what has changed it is the Industrial Revolution, bringing the railway and putting it within reach of the London commuter, so that, instead of brick-nog cottages and blacksmiths' shops, it is now a place of factories and supermarkets.

The multitude of chapels in Chesham's streets is one of the clues to the town's history, however, linking it closely with its neighbour Amersham in ecclesiastical matters, though the towns have been fierce rivals in secular affairs. A Lollard named Thomas Harding was burned at the stake here in 1532, and the town that now appears so conventional in fact has a long story of typical Chiltern unorthodoxy. The eccentric (some said insane) Roger Crabbe ran a hat-shop here after the Civil War and took to eating grass and dressing in sackcloth, saying he could live on three farthings a day. He was a bitter enemy of the local Quakers, though he shared with their founder an extensive repertoire of extravagant behaviour. Some believe he was the original of Lewis Carroll's Mad Hatter.

Amersham developed in a different way from Chesham, a fact for which we should be eternally grateful. Its modern growth took place separately, on the hill above the old town, so that the latter

Chenies — the Bedford Chapel.

The tomb of the second Earl of Bedford, Chenies. The alabaster monument to the Earl and his Countess, Margaret St John, was made by William Cure in 1619. Note the Earl's finely carved hands. Cure was paid £226.13.4d for this work.

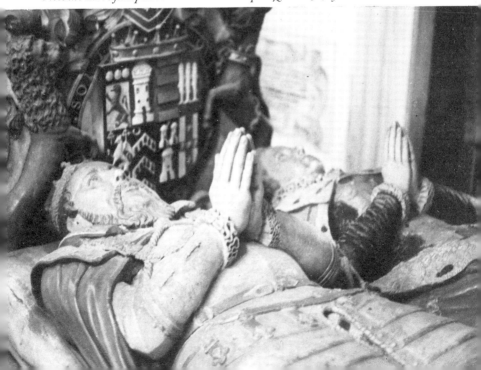

'The King's Arms', Amersham, undoubtedly the finest, but by no means the only fine frontage in the High Street, which sports a number of old coaching inns with arched entrances to their former stabling yards.

has been preserved more or less intact. Amersham-on-the-Hill, which the railway company itself dubbed 'Metroland', intending it as a compliment, when it brought the Metropolitan Railway out here, has nothing whatever to do with Chiltern country except that it occupies what was once Chiltern common land.

The wide High Street of old Amersham, however, despite its traffic-lights, mini-roundabouts and yellow lines, is one of the most delightful streets in the Chilterns. "A right praty market towne on Fryday," Leland called it, "of one strete well buildyd with tymber." A right pretty town any day of the week, I should say. Arched entrances to the coaching-inns still line the Aylesbury road, and it is not difficult to imagine these stabling-yards of old, with the clatter of hooves on cobblestones as shouting ostlers changed the horses for the next stage of the journey. The place has been variously called Elmodesham, Agmondesham and Amundesham, and if the latter should somehow remind us of the South

Pole, nothing, on the contrary, could be warmer and more welcoming than this splendid old town.

Amersham was the chief centre of Lollard activity in the Chilterns, and there is here a martyrs' memorial to William Tylsworth and others who were burned at the stake in 1506 on the instructions of the Bishop of Lincoln. It is said that Tylsworth's own daughter was forced to light the fire. These martyrs were not the first, or the last, in Amersham's story, but the site of the 1506 martyrdom was ascribed by tradition to a spot where no crops would grow. Science, however, found the barren soil to be due to a more mundane cause – an unusual formation of flints. Alas, Amersham's modern citizens are largely ignorant of this monument to their town's heroism. It is hidden away in the corner of a field, behind the garden of a house, and reached by a narrow, overgrown and unsignposted lane from Station Road. I asked a considerable number of people in the streets nearby to direct me to it. Only one of them had ever heard of it, and he, standing in Station Road not many yards from it, had no idea of its whereabouts.

Before this martyrdom, the Lord of the Manor of Chesham Bois, Sir Thomas Cheyne, whose family had given Chenies its

The Martyrs' Memorial, Amersham. Erected as a memorial to William Tylsworth and others who were burned at the stake by order of the Bishop of Lincoln in 1506, the monument is, by association, a tribute to all Chiltern martyrs who have died for the principle of freedom of conscience.

Amersham from Parsonage Wood — looking down on Old Amersham from the tively unspoiled town centres in England, old Amersham's

hillside above which the new town has grown. One of the most stylish and rela-
High Street is rich in Georgian houses.

Shardeloes. This house, now converted into luxury flats, was chiefly designed by Robert Adam, and built for William Drake, MP for Amersham, in 1766. The grounds were laid out by Humphrey Repton.

name, had supported the Lollard cause and was imprisoned for it, and religious dissent continued long afterwards to send ripples of disturbance over a widening radius from stones dropped on the surface of still waters at Amersham.

The Drake family, the local squires for three centuries, were true to form, even when religious disputes had become parlour-games for intellectuals. When the Penny Post in 1841 required houses to have numbers on their doors, Thomas Drake flatly refused to have London dictating what he did with *his* houses. The Drakes lived at Shardeloes, the white house standing on the hill outside the town towards Great Missenden. This Palladian mansion was originally designed by Stiff Leadbetter after an earlier house had been destroyed by fire, but it was completed by Robert Adam, and James Wyatt worked on the interior (a curious mixture of architects). The memorials to the Drake family are in Amersham's church of St Mary and are the finest collection in the Chilterns, next to those at Chenies.

Before getting lost in the real depths of the Chilterns, it will be as well to deal with the tongue of Buckinghamshire that pokes out, with justifiable rudeness, at London, and has Slough at its tip like a large pill which it is reluctant to swallow, having spit it out into Berkshire not long ago. This is the south-eastern fringe of the Chilterns most seriously affected by the capital's monstrous grasp, and, having looked at it, we shall then sensibly be retreating from London rather than advancing on it.

Two old villages called the Chalfonts are spread out along the River Misbourne below Amersham. Neither Chalfont St Giles nor Chalfont St Peter has much to offer the casual visitor, but the former is famous for a house a short distance from the village centre called 'Milton's Cottage'. Legend has it that the poet completed *Paradise Lost* here and began *Paradise Regained*, and the

Woodcarving at Chalfont St Giles. The pretty doorway of St Giles' Church is reached via an archway from the village street, and a swinging lychgate which naturally draws the local children like a magnet.

Milton's Cottage, Chalfont St Giles. Actually, the cottage was Thomas
Legend has it that he finished Paradise

Ellwood's. He lent it to Milton when the poet left London to avoid the plague. Lost here, and it is now a Milton museum.

cottage is kept as a Milton museum. It is a pretty enough cottage, to be sure, but it was not Milton's. It belonged to his Quaker friend Thomas Ellwood, who merely lent it to the blind poet for ten months in 1665 and the following year, to escape the plague then raging in London. Nor is there (alas for American tourists) any evidence to support the notion that he finished his greatest work in this house or began the other. Still, it is appropriate that Milton should have links with the Chilterns, for he was a somewhat notorious champion of English liberties in his time, in favour of divorce and passionately opposed to censorship.

Thomas Ellwood is buried at Jordans nearby, along with many other Quakers, including William Penn, the most famous and influential disciple of George Fox. The Friends' Meeting House, between Chalfont St Peter and Seer Green, was built in 1688. It is a simple and dignified building set in a peaceful spot near the village which has grown up there since the First World War. Old Jordans Farm, where the Friends used to meet before the Toleration Act permitted Dissenters to have their own places of worship, has a large barn said to have been built with timber from the *Mayflower*. G.K. Chesterton did not believe this story, and neither do I. It is a goofy notion invented by, or for, American tourists who do not know the difference between Fox's peace-loving Quakers and Calvin's zealous Pilgrim Fathers.

Affluent housing-estates link Chalfont St Peter with Gerrards Cross, and here is Buckinghamshire's largest Iron Age hill-fort. Just south of it is the point at which a more recent massive earth-work, the M40 motorway, enters the Chilterns.

The celebrated Burnham Beeches lie sandwiched between the motorway and the outskirts of Slough, but peace and ancient England are surprisingly well preserved here. The area is owned by the Corporation of London, which acquired it for use as a public open space for ever, and it contains the world's largest collection of ancient beeches, their average age being over three hundred years. The trees here include one which is thought to be the largest beech

The church at Gerrards Cross. Built in 1859, the church of St James was designed by Sir William Tite on rather Byzantine lines. It stands beside the A40 and, from this side, seems somewhat inaccessible for a church.

in England, called 'His Majesty', and an oak which stood here before Drake sailed round the world (although not so long before as to justify its name 'Druid's Oak'!).

The Hundred of Burnham was one of the original Chiltern Hundreds, and the Steward had a formidable task in preventing robberies in and around these dense woods. The locals regarded them as their own, and even at the end of last century, when the Corporation took over, they reacted violently against the new bye-laws, throwing the keeper into a pond. No wonder visitors carve their identities on these trees as they do on man-made ruins. They appear even older than they are, as if they flourished here when dinosaurs roamed the earth, and seem to offer immortality to the initials they bear.

Many of these old pollarded beeches are in the last stages of their lives, however. Deformed into grotesque shapes, their agonized torsos seem to be struggling for life like Laocoön in the Greek sculpture, and hollowed out by fungi, they can scarcely be called beautiful. Rather they are awe-inspiring and venerable ancients, whose cavernous trunks howl at Man's self-important brevity.

Their foliage has shielded many a famous head from the sun, among them Thomas Gray's and Sheridan's, Chopin's and Mendelssohn's. Sheridan and his bride Elizabeth Linley spent their honeymoon in a house at East Burnham, of which he wrote extravagantly to a friend: ". . . were I in a descriptive vein, I would draw you some of the prettiest scenes imaginable. From my account of East Burnham you will say that Paradise was but a kitchen garden to it". Chopin and Mendelssohn were later guests in the same house, when it was owned by the historian George Grote.

We have already touched on Cliveden, which entertained more powerful, if not more famous guests, but we might look at it more closely here, for it is one of the 'greatest' houses in the Chilterns, in the English sense of importance as well as in the American sense of

A veteran of Burnham Beeches. Ancient pollarded beeches of grotesque shape can be seen in these famous woods, still supporting growth despite their often cavernous trunks. This one may well have been growing here when Gray wrote his famous 'Elegy' not far away.

Cliveden. Built by Sir Charles Barry for the Duke of Sutherland, on the site of terrace can be seen the balustrade which the first

two earlier houses, Cliveden was given to the National Trust in 1942. Below the Viscount Astor brought here from the famous Villa Borghese in Rome.

size. Situated west of Burnham and north of Taplow, the mansion stands on a hill rising so steeply from the Thames that one of its owners called it a "precipice", and in fact the original name of the house was 'Cliffden'. The so-called Cliveden Reach is one of the best known stretches of the river.

The first house on the site was built for George Villiers, the second Duke of Buckingham, who also built Buckingham Palace. It was owned later by George Hamilton, Earl of Orkney, who married Elizabeth Villiers when the King had done with her, and after Orkney's death it was rented for some time by Frederick, Prince of Wales. Then it was burned down and rebuilt by Sir George Warrender, after whose demise the Duke of Sutherland bought it. Almost at once the house was burned down again, and the Duke set about building the present mansion, which was designed by Sir Charles Barry. The Duke of Westminster afterwards owned it for more than twenty years, before it was purchased from him in 1893 by William Waldorf Astor, the American millionaire who became a British citizen in 1899.

Astor was a man of more taste than the previous owners and made many improvements to the house and grounds, although, to my mind, the greatest service he *could* have performed would have been to demolish the hideously flamboyant clock-tower built after Barry's death by the Duke of Sutherland, which bears no conceivable relation to Barry's restrained design.

The Astors became one of the richest and most powerful families in England between the wars, when W.W. himself was made first a baron and then a viscount. They owned both *The Times* and the *Observer*; they had one member in the House of Lords and five in the House of Commons – including the first woman to sit there, Nancy Langhorne, Lady Astor, wife of the second Viscount – and if the old Cliveden had entertained George I, Garibaldi and Gladstone, the Astors were hosts to such as Churchill, Lawrence of Arabia and Joachim von Ribbentrop.

The irrepressible Nancy Astor was the most colourful among Cliveden's many owners, prodding Stalin, during a visit to Russia with her husband and Bernard Shaw, as fearlessly as she prodded Ribbentrop and Churchill at home. Churchill likened her first appearance in the House of Commons to having some woman enter his bath when he had only a sponge with which to protect himself. "Don't worry, Winston," Lady Astor told him, "you would be in no danger." After a stroke near the end of her life, she woke to find her children round her bed, and said: "Am I dying, or is this my birthday?"

The ignominious end of 'the Cliveden Set' has already taken up some space in this book, and it is sufficient to add here that the house was given to the National Trust by the second Viscount Astor in 1942 but remained the family home until the third Viscount died in 1966. It is now leased by the Trust to Stanford University but can be visited at certain times. The views of the Thames from the grounds are unrivalled, and one of the best is from an ancient propped-up tree called 'Canning's Oak', where that great statesman was fond of sitting when he was a guest here.

Moving north from Cliveden brings us to Wooburn (not to be confused with Woburn) and its extension, Wooburn Green.

Bank Holiday at Wooburn Green. The local populace gathers to witness a traditional tug-of-war on the ancient village green, less than a mile from the M40 motorway.

There is nothing specially worth pausing over for the tourist here, but Wooburn is notable for the fact that the Bishop of Lincoln, in whose diocese the village was, had a palace here, where much evil was done in the name of God. Men were murdered here or sent to the stake for their beliefs, and the demolition of the palace in the eighteenth century erased the edifice, but not the memory, of a religious tyranny which the Chiltern martyrs helped to destroy.

Beaconsfield lies on the other side of the motorway. The modern development is Metroland, but the Old Town is a miracle. In every street radiating from its centre there is spaciousness, something of real style and elegance, and scarcely a yellow line to be seen. The four main streets are called London End, Windsor End, Wycombe End and Aylesbury End, and every one of them is a priceless living museum of seventeenth- and eighteenth-century architecture, though London End starts ominously with the phoney façade of 'The Saracen's Head', one of a large number of coaching-inns within a small area, this having been a main stopping-place on the London to Oxford road.

Buried in the parish churchyard is Edmund Waller, that political poet of divided loyalties who addressed laudatory verses to both Cromwell and Charles II. Challenged by the King with the remark that the poem to him was inferior to Cromwell's, Waller said: "Poets, Sire, succeed better in fiction than in truth." A neat reply, but Waller was, in truth, the personification of Bunyan's Mr Facing-Both-Ways.

Benjamin Disraeli, on his elevation to the peerage, took his title from this town, in tribute to a famous orator who had come to live at Beaconsfield in 1768 and was buried in the parish church nearly thirty years later. Edmund Burke was the Irish son of a Protestant father and a Catholic mother, and the pupil of Quaker teachers, so it is hardly surprising that religious tolerance was one of his earliest principles, and freedom from oppression his characteristic platform. He spent most of his political career in opposition, where men such as he often serve their country best, campaigning against

Capel's House, Beaconsfield. This fine old house near the church was built around 1500, by a rector who had been left £40 in a will. Further down the lane is the Old Rectory, another superb old house.

the slave trade and the exploitation of India. But, with the revolution in France, his tolerance found its limits, and his famous book *Reflections on the French Revolution*, which ran into eleven editions within a year, provoked an equally famous response, Thomas Paine's *The Rights of Man*.

A rather different writer who lived here, arousing some controversy that was a storm in a buttercup, was Enid Blyton; and thinking of children's interests reminds me that just outside the town is the miniature village of Bekonscot, which has been growing there for fifty years and is now of such size, relatively speaking, that it has its own airport (thank goodness this is only fairyland and not reality). Its name is real, however, in the sense that its host town should be pronounced 'Bekonsfield' and not 'Beekonsfield'. We owe sufficient respect to this lovely old town of elegance and eloquence to pronounce its name properly.

G.K. Chesterton also made Beaconsfield his home for the last twenty-five years of his life and wrote his famous 'Father Brown' stories there. We are not far from *Noddy in Toyland* here, perhaps, but it is easy to underestimate G.K.C., whose initials were as instantly recognized in his day as those of G.B.S., with whom he conducted many a dispute in print, defending beef and beer, among other things, against Shaw's austere vegetarianism and total abstention. He was Shaw's only serious rival in the art of self-projection; his huge, good-humoured figure in cloak and pince-nez tending to swamp the deeply serious figure inside.

Chesterton was not entirely happy about moving to Beaconsfield. He did so because his wife wished it, but he was really a city man, like Dr Johnson, and it was a city man's mischievous jibe that got him sacked from the *Daily News* when he wrote some seemingly innocent verses about 'strange drinks'.

> Tea, although an Oriental,
> Is a gentleman, at least;
> Cocoa is a cad and coward,
> Cocoa is a vulgar beast,
> Cocoa is a dull, disloyal,
> Lying, crawling cad and clown . . .

The church of St Mary and All Saints, Beaconsfield. Heavily restored in the nine-teenth century, it is nevertheless prettily situated at the centre of the old town and contains the tomb of Edmund Burke.

Bekonscot. A splendidly entertaining model village which has been growing in Beaconsfield for the past fifty years.

The clue is in the repeated use of the word 'cad'. The owner of the *Daily News* was George Cadbury, of the Quaker chocolate family.

Chesterton habitually took his own drinks (I use the plural advisedly) at 'The White Hart', the seventeenth-century licensee of which was fined twopence for putting up a sign on waste ground some distance from the inn. It is still there, though not the original one, occupying space at the centre of Beaconsfield's traffic flow, where one would expect a concrete lamp-post, or a bus-shelter, or a public urinal.

At Penn, where the founder of Pennsylvania's ancestors came from (a stone in the church refers to him as 'Proprietor of Pennsylvania'), we are extremely close to the expanding Chiltern capital, but this village so far retains its own identity that Sir John Betjeman has called it "the Chelsea of the Chilterns". Its 'desirable properties', four village greens, monuments to the Penns and the Curzons in the lovely church of flint and old red brick, may easily

'The Royal Standard of England', Forty Green. Well known for its excellent cheese counter, this ancient country inn near Beaconsfield claims that Charles II spent one of his last nights in England hidden in the rafters.

Tylers Green. The boys are well-equipped for a long wait at the village pond. Tylers Green is a more-or-less modern extension of Penn and is separated from High Wycombe only by King's Wood.

give us a wrong impression of Penn, however, for it has in fact been one of the major centres of the chair-making industry next to High Wycombe itself.

High Wycombe's name is a piece of Chiltern irony, for the town, once known as 'Chepping Wycombe', signifying a market town (from the Anglo-Saxon 'cheapen'), lies along the deep valley of the River Wye. The main roads from north and south make such steep descents into the town that 'escape lanes' are necessary in case of brake failure. At its centre, the parish church, the old Guildhall and the market hall stand close together at one end of the High Street in a defensive huddle against the constricting advance of modernism. One or two other nice old buildings remain, converted into shops or banks, but the town is mainly a place of twentieth-century houses, factories, churches and public buildings, reflecting its fairly sudden transformation from a small Georgian market town into an industrial centre accommodating three-quarters of a million people.

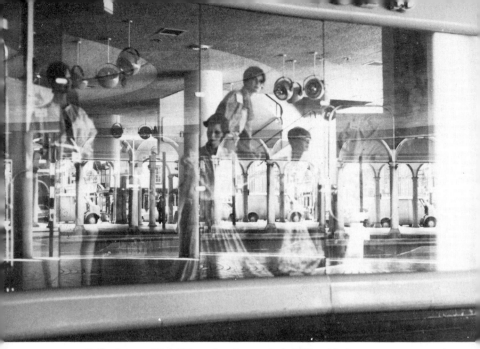

Reflections on High Wycombe. A couturier's fashionable dummies gaze out at the main street of High Wycombe through the Tuscan arcades of the Guildhall, built in 1757 by Henry Keene.

One of the town's more noticeable buildings is Wycombe Abbey School. It never was an abbey but was a manor house rebuilt in neo-Gothic style by James Wyatt for the first Baron Carrington in 1790. It became a girls' boarding-school a century after that and was soon famous, being sometimes called "the Eton of girls' schools".

High Wycombe preserves an estimable ancient ceremony whereby each year when a new Mayor is elected, the retiring and incoming Mayors are officially weighed at the Guildhall by the Chief Inspector of Weights and Measures. The object of the exercise was originally, of course, to determine whether the outgoing Mayor had lost weight through conscientious application to his duties or gained it by taking advantage of his office. Nowadays it is regarded as an amusing ritual, but it seems to be such a capital idea, and one that can be carried out with such little expense and inconvenience, that it ought to be extended to all those throughout the country who successfully seek public office.

Although it now has a wide variety of industry, High Wycombe's growth is based on furniture manufacture, carried on in a large number of factories, using vast quantities of imported timber. Two of the earliest manufacturers were Samuel Treacher and James Gomme. Treacher is said to have invented the Windsor chair, allegedly so called because George III had one and called it that. This tale is much disputed, however, and no one really knows the origin of the chair or its name. Gomme was the founder of the biggest and perhaps best-known company today, producing the famous G-Plan furniture. In 1811, during the period of extreme hardship and poverty caused by the Napoleonic Wars, he introduced a token coin for his workers, with his own name on it, which became known as the Bucks Shilling.

It would be extravagant to call Robert Adam 'a Chiltern Bob', but it was he who rebuilt the town's market hall (none too successfully) and, as well as Shardeloes, had a hand in the design of West Wycombe Park, towards which we will now progress.

The first-time visitor to West Wycombe village will be struck at once by the contrast with the town as he approaches on the straight road leading north-west from the town centre. The image of the sun on top of the church comes into view very early, and the road heads straight for it but comes first into the village street, which would be a delight if it were not for the constant stream of traffic passing through it. Most of this stylish and visually rewarding village, threatened with total demolition before the Second World War, is now owned by the National Trust. Church Loft, a fifteenth-century house with overhanging storey, admits one to Church Lane, climbing steeply towards St Lawrence's Church and the Dashwood Mausoleum. The faith of the villagers must have been strong for them to face this climb twice on Sundays, and one recalls Charles Churchill's comment:

> A temple built aloft in air
> That serves for show and not for prayer.

This is a misleading jibe, however, for the hill was an Iron Age hill-fort, and a village grew up on it called Haveringdon. There is

Looking towards High Wycombe. This is the view one gets standing directly in straight road to town was made at his expense,

front of Sir Francis Dashwood's mausoleum on West Wycombe Hill. The
using chalk from the caves beneath the hill.

Church Lane, West Wycombe: looking down towards Church Loft, the building with overhanging storey which disguises this charming lane from the village's main street.

still an Averingdown Farm a mile or so to the north. Not surprisingly, the village was eventually deserted for the more sheltered site below, but the thirteenth-century church remained there, an ideal subject for the exercise of Sir Francis Dashwood's odd and flamboyant mixture of paganism and Christianity.

The drive leading to West Wycombe House itself starts from the opposite side of the road. The mansion is one of the two or three finest in the Chilterns, and part of it is opened to the public on weekdays during the summer. Repton formed the lake by damming the River Wye. Nothing could be more innocuous than this colonnaded house and its grounds today, although the surviving Temple of the Winds still has a faintly phallic suggestion about it.

The mausoleum stands beside the church and commands a superb view of the road to High Wycombe, for which we have Sir Francis to thank. He bore the cost of re-aligning the road, ostensibly to provide work for the men of the village. But local gossips had it that he only wanted an excuse to excavate the caves under the hill, and logic is on their side, as there are obviously easier ways of quarrying chalk for a road than digging elaborate narrow tunnels deep into the hill. On the other hand, there are suggestions that caves existed here long before then, so Sir Francis may only have refined what was already here.

Whatever the truth of the matter, the legend remains that the Hell-Fire Club moved here when Medmenham became undesirable and that the caves were the scene of unspeakable orgies. Cashing in on the notoriety of their ancestor, therefore, the family installed electric lights and re-opened the caves in the 1950s and admits the public at a pound a head. In duty to this book, I paid up and went in. But these dimly-lit tunnels are no more than a children's amusement today, despite a recorded commentary by the present Sir Francis. Indeed, I would have thought that, as exciters of lust, they were always a flop. Nothing could be less evocative of the licentious revelry of eighteenth-century rakes, and stem the rise of passion more effectively, than these chilly, damp and dripping passages through the chalk.

Let us turn northwards into a space of a different sort. A glance at the map shows a large and relatively empty area bounded by High Wycombe, Chesham, Tring, Wendover and Princes Risborough, and at last, in entering this apparent wilderness, we can see some meaning in that ancient phrase "the deserts of Chiltern". The countryside is more open than to the south, and views across rolling hills with cornfields, sheep and cattle are more typical than dense beechwoods.

The delightful country around the scattered villages of Speen and Lacey Green seems like a different world from the more sophisticated towns and villages nearer London, and tucked away here at the junction of Pink Road, Lily Bottom Lane and Wardrobes Lane, not far from Loosely Row and Parslow's Hillock, is 'The Pink and Lily' public house, where a famous writer spent some happy weekends drinking beer, enjoying the surrounding landscape and composing verses. Was it Edward Lear or Lewis Carroll? No, the nonsense names deceive us. It was a more sensitive young Englishman, who is buried in a foreign field, but Rupert Brooke was quite equal to these associations, when the mood took him:

> . . . in that heaven of all their wish,
> There shall be no more land, say fish.

If one of the items in a sixteenth-century inventory of the property of Hawridge church — "one challis with the paten parshall gylt" — would seem to lend support to the idea of 'rustic simpletons' inhabiting this wilderness, there are other names that show us the countryman's no-nonsense forthrightness — the 'Maidenhead' at Cholesbury, and Bullbaiter's Lane at Hyde Heath — that was to breed powerful consequences for the whole of England.

If we follow Grim's Ditch northwards from near here, we shall come to Great Hampden, where there must once have been a village which has disappeared. Only a house with neo-Gothic battlements, a church and a farm remain, and it is difficult to imagine this peaceful countryside with its grazing sheep as a scene of revolution, but Hampden House, now a school, was the cradle of events which exploded into national issues that rocked England to its very

A roadsign at 'The Pink and Lily'. The casual visitor may well try to remember how many drinks he has had when he leaves the famous pub to find this sign facing him.

Great Hampden church. John Hampden is buried in this churchyard, but the exact
the

site of his grave is unknown. Hampden House, now a school, is behind the trees on right.

Landscape near Great Hampden: a typical scene in this part of Buckinghamshire, where pasture land stretches out between beechwoods capping the hilltops. The longest continuous stretch of Grim's Ditch starts near here.

foundations. This is true Chiltern country in both nature and spirit.

The family into which John Hampden was born in 1594 had been settled here since before the Norman Conquest. Queen Elizabeth had been a guest here of one of the wealthiest families of commoners in the land. John Hampden went to school at Thame and to university at Oxford, studied law and moved into politics as the burgess for Wendover, refusing to purchase his way into the House of Lords as his mother had wished him to do.

Gradually, over the years, representing the whole of Buckinghamshire as well as Wendover, he began to earn a reputation as an opponent of Charles I's illegal methods of raising taxes, and eventually – to escape persecution – he decided to emigrate to America with a fellow-Puritan, an unknown young cousin of his named Oliver Cromwell. Their ship was prevented from sailing, however. If the King had had the benefit of foreseeing the future, he would have been glad to let them go.

Charles issued a writ ordering the inland counties – contrary to the Petition of Right – to furnish men and money for the navy. Hampden's share was but a few paltry shillings he would not have noticed. But he saw a vital principle of English liberty at stake, and he refused to pay it, thus making himself the chief spokesman in the nation's grievances against the King. As Burke said, the payment would not have ruined his fortune, but it would have made him a slave. Hampden's Royalist opponents wanted to have him whipped, and it required a true hero's courage and conviction to stand firm as he did. Charles accused Hampden and his friends of high treason and burst into the House of Commons with an armed force to arrest them in person, but they had been forewarned and made themselves scarce.

This insult to Parliament was the worst and last blunder of Charles's reign. Four thousand Buckinghamshire men rode to London in support of their MP, who had been instrumental in abolishing Star Chamber and other evils during the famous Long Parliament. The Civil War was set in motion, and Hampden lost his life at Chalgrove, leading a force to intercept Royalist troops who had sacked Chinnor. His last words were, "O Lord, save my country."

If Hampden had lived, his moderation and incorruptibility *might* have saved the Commonwealth from its excesses. His refusal to pay the Ship Money put the final honourable nail in the coffin of the Divine Right of Kings, but the best that can be said of the immediate outcome is that it was a necessary evil.

It is one of the supreme ironies of the Chiltern story that the area, as one of the main centres of opposition to authority over a long period of English history, should have furthered the cause of that movement which has gradually destroyed the Chilterns' former character. For it is largely to the Puritans that we can trace the rise of capitalism* the consequences of which were the Industrial Revolution, the Enclosure Acts and the growth of mass-production that killed off the Chiltern craftsmen.

There is a greater irony yet, however. For this wild and untamed region of rebels and heretics has become the home of the

* See R.H. Tawney, *Religion and the Rise of Capitalism*

Bradenham — the church and manor house. Isaac d'Israeli, the antiquarian and father of Benjamin, lived here until his death in 1848. Educated at Leiden University, he wrote many books, his best-known being Curiosities of Literature; *his library served to educate his more famous son.*

chief representatives of stability and authority, the Prime Ministers of England. We shall come to Chequers presently, but in the meantime we are not far from Hughenden Manor, the home of Benjamin Disraeli, Earl of Beaconsfield. He was the son of Isaac d'Israeli, the antiquary, who lived at the nearby Bradenham Manor, where his son, though born in London, first grew to love the Chilterns. Benjamin was, in that strange phrase we still use, 'intended' for a career in law, but he turned to literature and produced a succession of novels before taking up politics.

There are some curious parallels in the careers of Disraeli and Sir Francis Dashwood. Both became Tory Members of Parliament for constituencies in Kent when they were thirty-three; both married wealthy widows shortly afterwards; both served terms as Chancellor of the Exchequer, and so on. We can hardly say that Disraeli was more orthodox than Sir Francis, since he was Jewish in race but not in religion, and radical by inclination but not by party. He was, in fact, a born cynic. But he was also a man of ambition, wit and intellect, which Dashwood was not. He said in a speech, soon after Darwin's *Origin of Species* burst upon the world: "The question is this: Is man an ape or an angel? My lord, I am on the side of the angels." Sir Francis, faced with the same question, would have delighted in siding publicly with the apes.

Disraeli and his wife bought Hughenden with her fortune in 1847 and lived there until their deaths, altering the former building into a showy and unattractive Gothic mansion, now owned by the National Trust. Meanwhile, Disraeli became Queen Victoria's Prime Minister. "Everyone likes flattery," he had said, "and when you come to royalty you should lay it on with a trowel." So he had her proclaimed Empress of India, and she, tit for tat, raised to the peerage her "kindest and most devoted" of ministers. After his death the Queen erected the memorial to him in Hughenden church, where he is buried.

Great and Little Missenden, taking their names from the little River Misbourne that trickles through them, lie alongside the main London-Aylesbury road which ran through Great Missenden until the by-pass was made in 1950, and the larger village has clearly suffered as a result of its centuries of traffic. The old road-sign still stands at the end of the village street, and other disfigurements —

Hughenden Manor. Disraeli lived here from 1847 until his death, 'ruthlessly dramatizing' the original house, according to Pevsner, who found the architectural details 'excruciating'. It is now owned by the National Trust and contains many relics of Lord Beaconsfield.

Little Missenden. One of many attractive cottages in this quiet and unspoiled village. The church has some ancient wall-paintings, and the village was the birthplace of Herbert Austin, the motor manufacturer.

double yellow lines among them — have made their appearance in a place which has paid the penalty of capitalizing on centuries of passing trade, while Little Missenden remains a stylish and attractive place which has been left in peace by stage-coach and automobile alike. The by-pass separated Great Missenden from its church, which is now reached by a footbridge across the main road, and that, too, is a sad comment on the capitalism that has made the larger village a mess whilst its neighbour still clusters cosily round its ancient place of worship.

A little north of Great Missenden is a village called The Lee, scattered and at first sight uninteresting, though if one approaches it via the corner where a huge ship's figurehead suddenly greets one, it can be a startling place, especially at night. The ship from which this came was bought by the Liberty family, who own the manor house here, and the oak beams were used in the famous Regent Street store founded by Sir Arthur Liberty. The family also built the village church — an uninspired red-brick building, but near it stands the original restored thirteenth-century chapel,

Apparition at The Lee. Representing Admiral Earl Howe, this ship's figurehead belonged to the training ship Impregnable, *formerly the* Howe, *which was sold to the Liberty family. The figurehead stands by the roadside and must have startled many a driver rounding the bend at night, whether drunk or sober.* **127**

with Cromwell and Hampden represented in the east window, and a font which could be locked to prevent witches from misusing the holy water.

The country round Chartridge, St Leonards and Cholesbury is fairly open rolling farmland, and there are plenty of lovely views from the ridges, but the small villages themselves are not distinguished. It is away from the modern building that this area is of interest. Grim's Ditch runs through the country towards Wigginton Bottom, and Bray's Wood, near The Lee, hides an ancient earthwork.

Near here is Asheridge Farm, which Aneurin Bevan bought in 1954. It has a lovely old farmhouse which Bevan made, as Michael Foot says, "a citadel against all political and newspaper invaders for the rest of his life". A familiar Chiltern story, and the true Chiltern spirit was present in this humanist from the Welsh valleys, drawing breath here before delivering one of his eloquent and passionate speeches or lambasting the Prime Minister as a man with "a genius for putting flamboyant labels on empty baggage". Bevan's monument is the National Health Service, and though it is now in need of urgent medical attention itself, it was probably that, more than anything else, which put the final nail in the coffin of witchcraft, in the Chilterns as elsewhere.

It is Cholesbury that guards some of the secrets of this countryside. The village church, like West Wycombe's, stands within a Belgic hill-fort known as Cholesbury Camp, on the summit of the ridge. The fort is about fifteen acres in extent and more or less circular in shape, and has double and triple ramparts on the eastern side. Hearths and pottery have been found there dating from the second century BC. We do not know very much about this settlement, but it is certainly curious that it lies half-surrounded by a wide arc of Grim's Ditch between Great Missenden and Berkhamsted. No more than coincidence, perhaps, since almost everyone denies that Grim's Ditch is prehistoric. Nevertheless, one wonders . . .

Across the ditch we come at last to Wendover, on the Upper Icknield Way. Its name is lovely, old and descriptive, and I, for one, do not agree with Robert Louis Stevenson, who found it a "straggling, purposeless sort of place". If only there were more places like it! In spite of the 'obvious' Englishness of Wendover's name, however, it should not surprise us that it is really Celtic, deriving from '*gwyn-dwfr*', meaning clear water or stream.

Wendover's fourteenth-century church lies nearly half a mile south of the little town's centre, and legend has it that witches moved it from its original site, still known as Witches' Meadow. The medieval historian Roger of Wendover was born here, and after becoming a monk at St Albans Abbey, where he died, he wrote a history of the world which is still valuable as an authority on his own times. Wendover has also sent distinguished representatives to Parliament in its time. As well as John Hampden, its MPs have included Burke and Canning.

The Upper Icknield going north-east from here climbs towards Tring via the huge Halton RAF Camp, and where the road turns east on to the A41 by Buckland Wharf, the next half mile of road at Tring Hill has been in turn the prehistoric Icknield Way, the Roman Akeman Street and the modern trunk road. The Lower

Wendover. The charming old town, with its clock tower at the bottom of the High Street, has many fine houses. Half way down on the right is 'The Red Lion', a heavily-timbered coaching inn at which Robert Louis Stevenson stayed.

The view from Coombe Hill: looking across the Vale of Aylesbury from

he highest point in the Chilterns, now owned by the National Trust.

Chequers, from the Ridgeway footpath. Let this photograph of the famous house be a warning to all amateur photographers – it cost me an embarrassing interview with a posse of the Bucks Constabulary, though I was on a public right-of-way.

Icknield, meanwhile, makes some quite extraordinary turns in and out of Aston Clinton and the attractive Weston Turville before rejoining the original route at World's End.

To the south-west out of Wendover, the Upper Way passes below Coombe Hill, the highest point in the Chilterns. There are spectacular views across the Vale of Aylesbury from this gorse-covered hilltop, which is now National Trust property. On a clear day the distant Cotswolds can be seen, and some say you can see St Paul's Cathedral in the opposite direction. I dare say you can if you really want to. The somewhat ill-fated monument on the hilltop is a memorial to the local men who died in the South African war. Erected in 1904, it was destroyed by lightning in 1938, then rebuilt. In 1972 the brass tablet was stolen from it, and that has now been replaced by a stone one.

Coombe Hill was presented to the National Trust by Lord Lee of Fareham, and it was also he who gave Chequers to the nation for the use of Prime Ministers. The Tudor mansion stands in its own little valley near Coombe Hill and Cymbeline's Mount (which is in its grounds) and takes its name from one Elias de Scaccario, a twelfth-century official who first owned the estate and whose Latin name was corrupted to de Chekers. Lady Mary Grey, of that unhappy Leicestershire family which included her sister, the Nine Days Queen, was made a prisoner here after offending Queen Elizabeth by marrying beneath her, and later the house was owned by descendants of Cromwell, many of whose relics are kept there in another piece of Chiltern irony – the veneration of relics having been one of the chief targets of Puritan aggression.

Prime Ministers from Lloyd George to the present have lived at Chequers and reacted in different ways to it. They, it might be supposed, need refuge from the turmoil of London more than most, but Bonar Law is said to have declined the use of Chequers because he disliked the country: he certainly disliked Lord Lee. Attlee, on the other hand, took to the area so much that he subsequently bought a house at Prestwood. Ramsay MacDonald called it "this house of comforting and regenerating rest", but Churchill characteristically took off into flights of rhetoric: "What distinguished guests it has sheltered, what momentous meetings it has witnessed, what fateful decisions have been taken under its roof."

Well, I had a momentous meeting of sorts there myself not long ago. I had intended writing to the Lord Privy Seal, as Chairman of the Chequers Trust, for permission to take a photograph of the house for this book. But before doing so I decided to walk up the Ridgeway footpath, which crosses the estate, to see if a satisfactory picture was available from there. I spent roughly ten minutes there and moved about eight paces off the public right-of-way into a cornfield to get a better angle. As I was returning to my car, I suddenly found a reception committee of police waiting for me, including an officer who appeared from behind and had clearly intended to cut me off if I had continued up the footpath instead of returning the way I had come. This man asked me if I had been in trouble with the police before. I *hoped* I was not in trouble with them *now*. Meanwhile, a WPC had taken down details of my identity which were radioed to their HQ for a check. Whilst waiting for the results, they showed some interest in the lens of my camera, and I enquired if they interviewed *everyone* who paused on the public footpath. They said not, but I had been there a few minutes. They had evidently seen my sunglasses glinting in the sunlight. ("Did you *know* it was Chequers?" one of them asked).

Ellesborough church: the Prime Minister's parish church. There is a record of oak posts being bought for the 'churchyard mound' here. 'Mound' is to be interpreted as 'fence' in the local dialect.

Eventually, I heard the man at the other end of the line say, "How tall is this chap?", and the answer to this apparently satisfied him. Content that I was not a security risk, they let me go, though showing a little anxiety – now that they believed my story about preparing a book on the Chilterns – that I should understand why they had to make these checks.

Well, of course, everyone understands that these officers were merely performing a necessary duty, but what interested me was the availability of details, including my height, which presumably came either from my National Service records or from my National Health Service details. I dare say that, if I should fall foul of the law in the future, a computer will throw up the ominous information that I was once interviewed by police for loitering near the Prime Minister's residence, and they will wonder if I am an anarchist. It seems to me rather important that the Ridgeway footpath should be re-aligned, keeping it clear of the Chequers estate. The photograph I took that day is not a particularly good picture, but after this experience it took on a special significance for me, so I have kept it in the book.

Chequers is in the parish of Ellesborough, and the village church is prominently situated north of Cymbeline's Mount, whilst a little

Painting in Little Kimble church. This fourteenth-century wall-painting of St George and the Princess is one of a number of such treasures in the small church of All Saints, which also contains tiles of even earlier date depicting figures from the Arthurian legends.

Monks Risborough. Fused now with its larger neighbour Princes Risborough, the village retains its old character around the church, where this picturesque row of cottages stands.

to the west are Great and Little Kimble, commonly supposed – though not by the experts – to have taken their names from Cymbeline. Magna lies on the Upper Icknield, Parva on the Lower. The larger church contains a copy of the document recording Hampden's refusal to pay Ship Money, for it was at a parish meeting in this church that the historic defiance occurred. It is the small and practically hidden church of Little Kimble that is a rare Chiltern treasure, however. Fading fourteenth-century paintings on the walls are the finest in Buckinghamshire, and include a very rare representation of St Francis talking to birds.

Coming to the Risborough gap, the Upper Icknield diverges from the main road to pass through Whiteleaf, which – quite apart from its famous cross – is an attractive and well-cared-for hamlet of old cottages. Below it lie Princes Risborough and Monks Risborough, now virtually joined together by modern expansion, whilst between Upper and Lower Icknield lies Askett, a hamlet distractingly pleasant to look at, but having, over the railway line, a hump-back bridge guaranteed to jolt the unwary motorist into concentration on the road.

Away across the other side of the Chilterns, the origins of the names Kings Langley and Abbots Langley are well documented, but in the case of Princes and Monks Risborough we are on less solid foundations. It is said that the Black Prince had a castle at the larger place and that the monks of Canterbury held the manor in which the smaller is situated, but both explanations are unproven. Certainly *someone* built a castle at what was then called Great Risborough, for its sparse remains have been found, but which particular prince it was we cannot be sure.

A lane near Princes Risborough leads to the church and few houses of Horsenden and then comes to nothing, so that this tiny village remains an exceptionally untroubled place only half a mile from railway station, housing estates and supermarkets. But Horsenden was once a village of more considerable size. Its church is only part of the original one, and all its old houses have disappeared. Was it a victim of the Black Death?

Princes Risborough church: fine Early-English triple-lancet windows in the south aisle. The shafts are of Purbeck marble. Much of the rest of this church has been restored in the nineteenth and present centuries.

Horsenden. Within throwing distance of Princes Risborough, this charming hamlet remains quiet and secluded. Whoever rediscovered the derelict hamlet and built the present houses did so with taste. Not least of its attractions is the dovecote behind this cottage.

Bledlow lies near the Lower Icknield, and on Wain Hill, above the village, is that other puzzling chalk cross, not as easily seen as Whiteleaf's, which looks rather like a space-rocket from here. An ugly line of pylons spoils the view across the vale, but between here and Bledlow Ridge is some of the best walking country in the Buckinghamshire Chilterns. The ground is dotted with Iron Age settlements, burial mounds and the sites of Roman villas and pockmarked with rabbit-holes. The hedgerows are often lined with cowslips, and it is said that nightingales sing where cowslips grow, while the views from the windswept ridge, which is not thickly wooded, are well worth the steady climb.

South of the ridge lie the curious hamlets collectively known as Radnage. The origin of this parish is obviously the hamlet by the simple church, but scattered widely around it are groups of houses variously known as Radnage Bottom, Town End, Bennett End, Radnage Common and – wait for it – The City! We might have smiled at the irony a few years ago, for these are among the most peaceful places in the entire Chilterns, but the M40 has come this way since then and streaks through the hills hardly more than a mile from the 'City' end of Radnage.

The motorway by-passes Stokenchurch, which sits astride the A40 and is dominated by the nearby Post Office tower, 320 feet high. Stokenchurch used to be in Oxfordshire and was one of the important centres of chair-making. The village's position high on the ridge ought to make it an attractive place, but it is traffic-bound and neglected.

Ibstone, on the other side of the motorway, is spread along a road from its common towards Turville, and its interesting little church is some way to the south, standing at a corner where the road dips down and – when the hedges are cut – providing a tempting glimpse of the valley below. What this scene promises, it delivers in abundance. The square mile enclosing Turville, Fingest and Skirmett is the epitome of Chiltern landscape, and I would unhesitatingly pinpoint this group of villages as the very heart of all the Chilterns. Lazing together in a secluded and languorous maze of little valleys, each village has its separate identity, but the group together is Eden and Arcadia rolled into one.

Turville, protected by single-track roads, is the photogenic one. An old smock-mill, converted to a dwelling-house, stands sentinel on the hill above it, and its pretty cottages and narrow lanes lead off the green where church and inn – 'The Bull and Butcher' – stand, as if they had been together there since the beginning of time. There is nothing remarkable about any one of its buildings (Pevsner refers to its "jolly" vicarage); its beauty consists in its natural evolvement around the green. It does not have that artificial quaintness that presents its made-up face to the still-photographer like a prima donna, yet it is no surprise to learn that it has been used for filming. It is a place of oak beams and ingle-nooks and flint walls, where bees grow drowsy on the nectar of roses, and swallows show off their high-speed aerobatics round the roofs of thatch and tile.

Fingest is, to my eye (though I am in a minority), even more at-tractive. Massingham deplored the modern building going on

A corner of Turville. 'Quaint' is not a favourite word of mine, but if it can be usea
and the Bull ana

of any Chiltern village, it must be Turville. These cottages are near the church
Butcher Inn.

The church at Fingest. The famous twin saddle-back roof of St Bartholomew's is much later than the Norman original, but the scene epitomizes the timeless quality of the best Chiltern landscapes. To the right of the meadow is the village cricket field, and on the hill, Mousell's Wood.

Fingest from Hanger Wood: looking across Manor Farm to one of the most delightfully typical English villages in all the Chiltern country, nestling in its own valley, surrounded by beechwoods on the hillsides.

there and said: "Let Fingest go since it is doomed, if only we can keep Turville." But we cannot put our living villages in a deep freeze, and Fingest seems to me, despite its changes, to have a quality of timeless tranquillity that makes it appear 'natural' and not man-made at all. It has heard the shrieks of childbirth, sighs of love, shouts of anger, agonies of death – like other villages. The ecclesiastical court in 1519 ordered one John Plumrige to do bare-footed penance in this church for making his wife pregnant before they were married, and more recently the village was the home of that arch-exponent of urban invective the *Daily Mirror*'s 'Cassandra'. (As for Turville, it is the scene of unsolved murder.) Perhaps, like much else in English life, the difference between appearance and reality is a kind of hypocrisy, but Fingest is one of those rare places that seem superior to the sum of the human beings who make them, and if you wanted to show a foreigner a place with all the qualities we know as 'Englishness' without knowing how to define it, you could hardly beat bringing him to Fingest.

The view of the village from the hillside on the west flank of Hanger Wood, looking over Manor Farm, is without equal, and well worth the fairly steep climb. Only birds, and the crack of cricket bat on ball, or the mellow tone of the church bell on a Sunday, are likely to disturb this peaceful and superb vantage point. The Norman church tower, with its rare twin saddle-back roof (the experts call it 'bifurcated', but then experts have ugly

names for everything), was surely never erected by such beings as masons and labourers but grew out of the soil before the Romans, before the Celtic wanderers came here, and has merely been used for a church, as the adjacent meadow has for a cricket field.

I move on reluctantly from this blissful sanctuary, past Frieth and towards the Thames valley, and a place of much greater fame and popularity, Marlow. The little town has undeniably retained some style, due in no small measure to the active Marlow Preservation Society, but it is, alas, a place of noise and crowds, coaches and double yellow lines, which bury its attractions beneath the flourishing Admass.

Thomas Love Peacock wrote *Nightmare Abbey* here in West Street and entertained Shelley and his new wife, Mary, and they subsequently took a long lease on a damp house here but stayed less than a year, having to go to Italy for the sake of Shelley's health. The atheistic Shelley – regarded as a villain by the Establishment (who took exception to his habit, among other things, of reading a book whilst walking to the shops) – was another kindred spirit of Chilternism. His famous lines from 'Prometheus Unbound' might almost have been the text for the Chiltern martyrs:

> To suffer woes which Hope thinks infinite;
> To forgive wrongs darker than death or night;
> To defy Power, which seems omnipotent;
> Neither to change, nor falter, nor repent;
> This . . . is to be
> Good, great and joyous, beautiful and free;
> This is alone Life, Joy, Empire, and Victory.

Shelley was happy here, calling himself 'the Hermit of Marlow', making visits on foot to Great Hampden, Medmenham Abbey and Cliveden, walking in the woods at Bisham and sailing on the river, in days when Marlow was quieter than it is now. Mary Shelley was pregnant, and she gave birth to their daughter here, but while her husband worked on his great poem, 'The Revolt of Islam', she completed her famous fantasy *Frankenstein*, having had the idea in Switzerland when Byron had proposed that each of them should write a ghost-story to pass the time.

Marlow church from Clark's Bridge. The suspension bridge was designed by William Tierney Clark, who later built a similar but larger one across the Danube at Budapest. Marlow's has been threatened with demolition as a bottleneck, but happily survives.

Strictly, this town is Great Marlow, for a mile to the east is Little Marlow and, as if these places were some kind of Mecca for thriller-writers, buried in the churchyard is that prolific novelist and inveterate gambler Edgar Wallace, who started as a newspaper-boy and finished as the Chairman of the British Lion Film Corporation.

When Daniel Defoe came this way, early in the eighteenth century, he remarked that Great Marlow "is a town of very great embarkation on the Thames, not so much for goods wrought here (for the trade of the town is chiefly in bone-lace) but for goods from the neighbouring towns, and particularly, a very great quantity of malt, and meal, is brought hither from High-Wickham". Defoe also observed that "a vast quantity of beech wood, which

Hambleden Mill. The white-boarded mill on the Thames is a favourite calendar subject, and the village itself, a pleasant one-mile walk away, is among the prettiest in the Chilterns.

grows in the woods of Buckinghamshire" was sent from here to the capital, "without which, the city of London would be put to more difficulty, than for any thing of its kind in the nation".

Up-river is Medmenham – only a church and a string of houses leading straight to the river bank, but behind them was St Mary's Abbey, converted into a mansion where Hell-Fire Dashwood and his Monks had their sinister gatherings. It is now thoroughly respectable – it belongs to the Ministry of Defence.

Still further up-stream is Hambleden Mill End, with its picturesque old mill by the racing water, and, turning 'inland' again, the attractive village of Hambleden itself, where the churchyard contains the grave of one who made much profit out of the Shelleys and Wallace, and whose descendants will hopefully make a little bit out of me. His name was W.H. Smith.

Hambleden has a ghost, too. Mary Blandy is said to ride a white horse along one of the lonely roads near the village. (Are phantom horses always white, on the grounds that you would not be able to see a black one in the dark?) Mary was executed at Oxford in 1752 for the murder of her father – a wealthy lawyer – by arsenic poisoning, after he had forbidden her lover to enter their house at Henley. There was a great deal of public sympathy for her, and she became popularly known as 'the murdered maid'.

Round the bend of the river, and in the very corner of Buckinghamshire, is Fawley Court, former home of the Freeman family, who built most of the village church some distance away. Fawley Court is now a Catholic college. Names such as Christopher Wren, Grinling Gibbons, James Wyatt and 'Capability' Brown are much bandied about in connection with Fawley, but the contributions of Wren and Gibbons, at least, seem to be no more than undocumented attributions, and doubtful ones at that. When one looks at the hefty and artless mausoleums of the Freemans and the Mackenzies in the churchyard, it is difficult to imagine that *any* worthy artist had a hand in their affairs, and it is a blessing that these solid structures are almost hidden by the trees. What can be said with certainty is that this corner of the Buckinghamshire Chilterns is a secluded and unknown place, and from it we cross into an equally secreted corner of Oxfordshire.

Beeches in Maidensgrove Woods. A typical hillside beech coppice in the Oxford-shire Chilterns, where the woods become more dense and luxuriant towards the Thames valley. Note the lack of undergrowth.

148

CHAPTER 4

THE HEAD:

OXFORDSHIRE

The west side of the B40 road from Henley to Watlington is Oxfordshire, and across from Fawley we can immediately find, within a quite small area, much of the county's fascinating Chiltern character. Some say the Oxfordshire Chilterns are the finest part of the hills. It is an opinion I do not entirely share, but there is undeniably much secluded beauty in this most densely wooded section of the region.

Running north from the village of Bix is a narrow lane leading to Bix Bottom, Valley Farm and nowhere; tucked away among the trees are the crumbling ivy-covered walls of the little church of St James. This must have been at the centre of the original village when it was built, some seven or eight hundred years ago, but the population evidently migrated up the slope, or the 'pitch' as it would be called here, to the roadside. The church was finally abandoned in 1875 when the new one was built. As I approached the hidden ruin, I heard a murmur that I fancied was the ghost of some long-dead incumbent, spreading the gospel to a congregation of sparrows, but it turned out to be the local apiarist's beehives, standing among the gravestones which lay beneath the grass and nettles.

Beyond Maidensgrove Scrubs lies Stonor, with its well-screened Elizabethan mansion in a large deer park, the ancestral home of the Stonor family whose heads are the barons Camoys, one of whom led the left wing of the English army at Agincourt. The house contains some of the county's earliest brickwork.

The Roman Catholic Stonor family has been associated with Stonor Park since the thirteenth century and belongs to the Chilterns in spirit as well as in body, for, although its faith is not that of most Chiltern martyrs and heretics, it has been much persecuted for it. Edmund Campion, the Jesuit priest, was given refuge here in the sixteenth century by Dame Cecilia Stonor, who stood to lose everything by harbouring him. Before his arrest, torture and execution, Campion set up a secret press in order to print attacks on Protestants and boost the morale of the persecuted Catholics. The Chilterns are admirably impartial in their protective embraces.

The parish in which Stonor is situated is Pishill, the name of which does not, we are assured, mean what it seems to mean, although it has always been spelled thus. It actually means 'hill where peas are grown', according to the place-name experts. Nevertheless, a fellow named Wiggins was brought before the church court in 1811 for "making a Privey neere the Churchyard", and there is some mystery about how Russell's Water got to be where it is.

Arthur Mee, that high-minded surveyor of the King's England, could not bring himself to mention Pishill, and he associated Stonor with Bix, but the living of Pishill was once the Stonor family's responsibility, and they feared excommunication if they failed to appoint a curate, even though they had their own private chapel in the house. One incumbent was suspended for performing illegal marriages in Pishill church, which now contains a stained-glass window by John Piper, who lives in the Chilterns not far away.

Russell's Water is one of the occasional examples of a hilltop village pond apparently lying on porous chalk, where we should hardly expect to find it. The water-supply to high-ground settlements was a constant problem in the Chilterns before the introduction of mains water. The digging of wells was a difficult undertaking – often an impossible one, and natural springs were

Russell's Water. I have not discovered who Russell was, but his Water is the duckpond of this hamlet in some of the most remote and unspoiled Chiltern country.

few and far between. It is one of the reasons for sparse settlement in the hills. In some places, however, the chalk is overlaid with clay, so that rainwater ponds have formed naturally, and elsewhere ponds were dug by the local people and lined with clay bonded with straw. However they were formed, the Chiltern ponds are centuries old.

Four miles to the south-west is a more bizarre reminder of the water problem on the chalk uplands. The Maharajah of Benares was told, by the Governor of the Indian North-West Provinces, Edward Reade of Ipsden, about Stoke Row's problem in obtaining water, and the Prince generously undertook to remedy the problem by providing a well. The Maharajah's Well is 368 feet deep and was completed in 1864. Surmounted by an oriental cupola, it looks rather like a bandstand and distinctly out of place among the village's council houses.

So does the restored and preserved brick-kiln at Nettlebed,

The Maharajah's Well, Stoke Row. The cupola covers a well dug at the expense of the Maharajah of Benares, who was told of the village's difficulty in obtaining water. (Whipsnade is not the only place in the Chilterns with an Indian elephant — one stands above the winding-gear.)

Brick kiln, Nettlebed. This has been preserved as a monument to Nettlebed's ancient industry of brick-making. The old bricks are rather more attractive than those in the modern houses surrounding it.

Ewelme from Rabbits Hill. Mellow brick buildings and a stream with watercress beds characterize this village – certainly one of the most attractive and fascinating in the Chilterns, lying at the foot of the escarpment in Oxfordshire.

clean as a new pin and standing erect amid a modern housing-estate like a phallic exhortation to the local newly-weds. The village's brick-making industry began in the fifteenth century, however, and supplied the materials for some of the earliest brick buildings in Oxfordshire. Nettlebed now suffers very much from the fact that it stands at the junction of two main roads through the area, but it is surrounded by beautiful beechwoods.

The Reade family of Ipsden produced a son better known than the Maharajah's friend. Charles Reade was born at Ipsden House in 1814 and, after studying at Oxford and being called to the Bar at Lincoln's Inn, turned to literature instead of practising law. His most famous work is his romantic novel *The Cloister and the Hearth*, but he is scarcely read nowadays, being somewhat melodramatic, like most Victorian novelists.

Nuffield has a proud and famous name that the village's unassuming nature would hardly lead us to expect, for William Morris, the motor-manufacturer, took his name from it when he was raised to the peerage. Lord Nuffield's enormous philanthropic enterprises made this small Chiltern village's name known throughout the world, not only in the motor trade but in medical research, education, social studies and other important fields. He is buried beneath an unpretentious gravestone in the churchyard.

A well-preserved stretch of Grim's Ditch runs west from near the church, which is of Norman origin and has Roman tiles built into its walls. When I was last there, potatoes were growing beside the east wall. The Ridgeway path runs alongside the ditch here, and from a field near the church the six cooling-towers of the Didcot Power Station are a prominent feature of the Oxfordshire plain below.

The ditch is crossed by the Icknield Way, which comes north from Ipsden via Drunken Bottom, and following this we come towards Ewelme, another real peach of a village just on the fringe of the Chilterns. Built round its pretty, battlemented church, Ewelme contains a group of medieval buildings unique in their surviving unity, surrounded by old cottages, near which a clear stream trickles through watercress beds. Some say this village is the prettiest in all the Chilterns. It is certainly the most fascinating. Right across on the opposite side of the hills from Chenies, it contains the finest man-made treasure of the Chilterns since we left the Bedford Chapel.

Ewelme's story begins with illustrious names – Geoffrey Chaucer and Joan of Arc. The siege of Orleans in 1428, during the Hundred Years' War, was led by Thomas Montacute, Earl of Salisbury, who was killed when the Maid of Orleans rallied the French troops and led them against the English. Salisbury's widow was Alice Chaucer, granddaughter of Geoffrey and his wife Philippa. Thomas Chaucer, the poet's son and Alice's father, had fought at Agincourt and married Matilda Burghersh, who inherited the manor of Ewelme from her father.

Before Joan of Arc was brought to the stake at Rouen, Countess Alice had married again. Her second husband was the ambitious William de la Pole, Earl of Suffolk, who was soon made Duke by the young Henry VI. Largely responsible for organizing the marriage of the feeble Henry and the redoubtable Margaret of Anjou, Suffolk quickly became the King's favourite, and his wife the Queen's, and for a time the Suffolks held the fate of the country in their hands.

The tomb of Duchess Alice, Ewelme. The fabulously rich carving of the tomb of Alice, Duchess of Suffolk, who died in 1475, makes this one of the most priceless of Chiltern treasures. But below the tomb-chest is a macabre Gothic 'Memento Mori' to remind us that life is not to be taken for granted, even by a duchess.

Shakespeare subscribes to the notion that Suffolk had fancied the fifteen-year-old Margaret himself:

> She's beautiful, and therefore to be woo'd;
> She is a woman, therefore to be won.

And he has Suffolk saying:

> Margaret shall now be queen, and rule the King;
> But I will rule both her, the King and realm.

It is widely believed that Suffolk was responsible for the death of his political rival, Humphrey, Duke of Gloucester.

Meanwhile, he and Duchess Alice feathered their nest and began the building of the model village of Ewelme, around the palace, church, school and hospital for thirteen poor men. The buildings were not completed until after the Duke's death, in 1450, but, except for the palace, which has disappeared, they remain together and in use today.

The Duke of Suffolk's deep involvement in the loss of France created a national scandal which the King heeded by sending Suffolk abroad for safety, but the Duke had hardly set sail when he was seized and thrown into a small boat, where his head was unceremoniously hacked off with a rusty sword and chucked over the side, followed at once by his body.

The wealthy and twice-widowed Alice retired here to Ewelme and completed her buildings, surviving her husband by twenty-five years, and when she died, she was buried in this church in a superb alabaster tomb which is the chief, though far from the only, treasure of this village. Her effigy lies in all its finery, her head on a pillow of alabaster beneath a finely-carved stone canopy. She wears her coronet and the Order of the Garter and has angels all about her. The tomb rests on open arches, and the irony of this noble lady's magnificence can be glimpsed in the dark shadows beneath her monument. For there is the alabaster cadaver of the seventy-one-year-old Duchess, a half-naked and emaciated corpse, to remind us that, for all her and her husband's rapacious accumulation of wealth and power, she is but a dead old woman just like the poorest parishioner in the churchyard outside. And the fame of the village, as opposed to the welfare of its old men and its children, rests not with Duchess Alice but with the unknown craftsman who carved her monument.

The buildings, however, attest to that need to do good works, born of the medieval terror of retribution after death, which was able to co-exist quite happily with the most unabashed avarice during life, just as the effigy on the tomb, by joining her hands in prayer, contrives to make Duchess Alice look holy, as well as rich.

The almshouses, reached by steps leading from the west door of the church, are the oldest surviving brick buildings in the Chilterns, and the school is the oldest free Church of England school in the country, the Duke and Duchess having founded it for the education of the village children "freely, without exaccion of any schole hire".

A pig-farm near Britwell Salome. In the background is Britwell House, built in the eighteenth century by the Catholic lord of the manor, Sir Edward Simeon.

Britwell Salome, further along the Icknield Way, is remarkable only for its curious name, which conjures up visions of more severed heads and more alluring nakedness, but alas, the only seven veils here are the centuries obscuring the name's real origin, from the thirteenth-century lord of the manor, Almaric de Suleham.

Watlington is next, with its old brick Town Hall, and below it a market hall, at its centre. This was built by Thomas Stonor of Watlington Park in 1665. Watlington was an important market town once and could boast a variety of craftsmen serving the surrounding farms and villages – saddlers, braziers, coopers and thatchers, wheelwrights and millwrights. Now it is a quiet place, known more for the hill above it, with the white mark on it, than for the little town itself. It is still, architecturally speaking, a most interesting place, however, with some nice Georgian buildings, and well worth pausing in.

We lose track of the Lower Icknield Way just beyond Watlington. It cannot have just petered out. Perhaps it continued to

Ewelme once and then rejoined the Upper Icknield as the road approached the river on lower ground. Watlington Hill is National Trust territory, with good views from the top, and the road up it leads to Christmas Common, so called, according to legend, because Royalists and Parliamentarians arranged a temporary truce here for the Christmas of 1643.

We are again in the splendid walking country along the western edge of the Chilterns here, with Swyncombe Downs to the south-west of Christmas Common and Wormsley Park to the east. Swyncombe's little Norman church is near the manor house tucked away in a quiet lane. The rectory here was built by Daniel Harris, a local man who combined his post as Keeper of Oxford Gaol with occasional excursions into architecture, and took his convicts with him to work on his building projects!

Watlington – the Town Hall. It was built in 1655 by Thomas Stonor as a grammar school with market hall beneath. It has been altered a little since, but it still stands in the middle of the square. If it were demolished, it would inevitably be replaced by multiple traffic-lights.

The peaceful solitude of this area is the haunt of birds and deer and botanists – whole secret wildernesses of tilting woods and rolling hills where there is hardly a building, let alone a road. The mixed forest of Cowleaze Wood has a fine show of bluebells in the spring.

Among the trees near its church, Shirburn hides a medieval fortified house known as Shirburn Castle, which is certainly among the oldest brick buildings in the county. It was acquired by Thomas Parker, first Earl of Macclesfield, in the eighteenth century. Standing in its own park and surrounded by a moat, it is said (I have not seen it) to have battlements, towers, drawbridges and a portcullis but has been so altered by succeeding owners that it no longer possesses the romantic aura one would expect.

The Earl became George I's Lord Chancellor and read the King's speeches from the throne (since the King could not speak English). He was a keen amateur astronomer and a friend of Sir Isaac Newton. But, like his distinguished predecessor in office Sir Francis Bacon, he made enormous profits from his position and was at last found out and convicted of corruption.

His son the second Earl, also an astronomer, helped to frame Lord Chesterfield's Bill for the Adoption in Britain of the Gregorian Calendar in 1752. This was nearly two hundred years after it had been brought into use by the Catholic countries of Europe, because Protestant England had no intention of being told what time it was by the Pope. When the measure did become law, it led to riots because people jumped to the conclusion that the government was shortening their lives by eleven days.

Lewknor used to be described in the guide-books as a pretty village, but it is not particularly so today, and it has the M40 screaming past it as it leaves the Chilterns behind on its urgent way to Oxford. It was a merciful end, no doubt, that denied H.J. Massingham a long enough life to see this serpent of modernity streaking through his beloved Chilterns. How he would have raged against the fools of Whitehall who allowed – indeed *insisted* on – its coming this way. But more of that later.

Chinnor is the northern limit of the Oxfordshire Chilterns, and that, too, is hardly a pretty sight now, though it apparently was

A timber-yard at Chinnor. Dealing in timber is still an important Chiltern indus-try, supplying furniture-manufacturers here and elsewhere, but though locally-grown beech and other trees are still used, a great deal of foreign timber is imported nowadays.

once. It lies on the Icknield Way below Bledlow Cross, and this stretch of 'Acklin Street', as it was called locally, was notorious in the Middle Ages for the high incidence of murder, rape and rob-bery. Birds nest in the gargoyles of Chinnor's ancient church, which contains some fine brasses and an image of St Alban in one of its original windows. But Chinnor has become industrialized and over-developed and is an ugly place today, dominated by its huge cement-works covering a large area where once one of the village's open fields was cultivated. It is entirely sacrificed to the need for local employment. Let us hasten back to the more secluded area where we first turned north.

Near Stoke Row is Checkendon, an unremarkable village except for its Norman church, a fine building with a rounded apse, standing at the corner of the village green. It has one of the largest collections of brasses in Oxfordshire. In spite of its modern trap-pings (Massingham referred to "an altar-cloth that would disgrace

The church of St Peter and St Paul, Checkendon. Witches are said to have moved this church to a different site from the one planned, but whatever its situation, it is one of the most attractive Chiltern churches. Norman arches lead into the apse with steps up to the altar.

Memorial in Checkendon church. This memorial to Herbert and Maude Roth-barth is by Eric Kennington and is described (unfairly, I think) as "elephantine" in Pevsner's Oxfordshire. *There is a memorial window to Kennington himself, who encouraged local craftsmen to carve the church's new roof.*

Above: *Ruins of the original Greys Court, the picturesque remains of the forti-fied house of the de Grey family, built of flint and brick, the brickwork being certainly some of the earliest in Oxfordshire.* Below: *Greys Court, Rotherfield Greys, built by the Knollys family in the sixteenth century. Robert Carr, Earl of Somerset, and his wife Frances were kept here in the custody of Sir William Knollys, Viscount Wallingford, after their conviction for the murder of Sir Thomas Overbury.*

the rites of a Solomon Islander"), it is a church of great charm, with two Norman arches leading into the apse and steps to the altar – a little church as dignified in its simplicity as Chenies or Ewelme are in their lavishness.

If we go beyond Woodcote from here we are heading back towards the plain, and in that direction and around Ipsden the effects of modern farming methods can be seen, with trees and hedges torn up to create large arable fields that can be worked economically with the most up-to-date machinery. But if we turn eastwards from Checkendon, we penetrate the thickest beech-woods above the Thames, the very opposite of the empty plains below.

Rotherfield Greys and Rotherfield Peppard lie among the lovely sloping hills, their common Saxon name meaning cattle-grazing land, and their second names those of the two families who shared it. Across the bottom below Rotherfield Greys is Greys Court, a Stuart house now owned by the National Trust. The de Grey family – one of whom offended the king by drawing a dagger in the monarch's presence – built the original castle there, only fragments of which remain, this having been superseded by an Elizabethan mansion built by the Knollys family. Between the Greys and the Knollyses the place was owned by the Lovels, who forfeited the estate to the Crown when one of them, who had been a friend and henchman of Richard III, joined the Simnel plot against Henry VII. It was this Francis, Viscount Lovel, who was named in the lines published in London in 1484 which got their instigator hanged, drawn and quartered:

> The cat, the rat, and Lovel our dog,
> Rule all England under an hog.

The cat was Sir William Catesby, the rat Sir Richard Ratcliffe, and the hog King Richard.

The first of the Knollys line here was Sir Francis, who had Mary, Queen of Scots, in his charge at Bolton in Elizabeth's reign, but the subsequent family history did not endear the Knollyses to their monarchs, either. During the Civil War, the house was wrecked and the present one built in its place. The Tudor stables remain, however, as does the well-house, where the well, two hundred feet deep, was operated by a donkey treading a large wheel which is the largest surviving example in England. In the gardens, ancient wisterias coil round their supports like primeval serpents.

Rotherfield Peppard, whose church has a chequered tower of flint and stone supporting a spire, unusual in the Chilterns, is separated from the modern build-up of Sonning Common only by the fifty-six acres of Peppard Common, an attractive area preserved by the Nettlebed and District Commons Conservators. Peppard was the unlikely scene of an affair between Bertrand Russell and Lady Ottoline Morell.

The ground to the east drops down to the river again, and Henley-on-Thames waits to greet us, as indeed it waits to greet everybody. Henley's right to be called a Chiltern town is questionable, but if we give it the benefit of the doubt, we have to admit at once that this town in summer is the busiest and most impenetrable tourist attraction we have encountered since we left Whipsnade Zoo. Its famed regatta has been held in the first week of July since 1839, and during this period you can hardly see the water for the boats, or the boats for the people.

The main Chiltern road into Henley, from Nettlebed, descends through splendid beechwoods, and the minor road from Greys Court joins it where it turns towards the church and the famous bridge over the river. The bridge was designed by William Hayward, and on its keystones are images of Father Thames and Isis, sculpted by the eccentric Anne Seymour Damer and somewhat extravagantly praised by her cousin Horace Walpole, who left Strawberry Hill to her when he died. The bridge was the most important structure here for centuries, since the town's livelihood depended on it. There has been one here since the thirteenth century, and the present one was erected in 1786 after its predecessor had been destroyed by flooding.

Henley's oldest buildings – as difficult to see as the river in regatta week, because of heavy bombardment by traffic – include a Chantry House behind the church, inns with their old bear-baiting yards, and houses with timbers taken from old men-o'-war, as well as malting kilns which have been used in the chief in-

A barn at Harpsden. The end wall, with two others nearby, is made up of old wallpaper-blocks brought here by the lord of the manor from a wallpaper-factory in London.

dustry of a town described in its Victorian days as one of the neatest and cleanest in Oxfordshire. Among the other interesting buildings is the Kenton Theatre in New Street. Built in 1805, the year of Trafalgar, it is one of England's oldest surviving theatres.

Just outside Henley to the south is Harpsden, and, a little further upstream, Shiplake. Both are remarkably quiet villages so close to the bustling and overcrowded Henley. Harpsden's church stands between a gabled Tudor mansion, Harpsden Court, and a farm which – for a change – has the village's most curious architectural ornament. The timber barns catch your eye as soon as you enter the village, for their end walls are made up of square wooden blocks which were once used to print patterns on wallpapers, before the introduction of modern printing and embossing techniques.

Shiplake is well known as the scene of Tennyson's marriage to Emily Sellwood, a fortnight after the publication of 'In Memoriam'. In the same year he succeeded Wordsworth as Poet

Henley-on-Thames. A bridge across the river here has been an important factor in arch has a head on each side, one of Father Thames and the other of

Henley's prosperity for centuries. The present one was built in 1786. The central
Isis, the latter being the old name for the upper reaches of the river.

Laureate. The church has since undergone much rebuilding, but its windows retain some superb medieval glass which the poet and his bride saw, brought here in 1830 from the Abbey of St Bertin in France.

Not so well known is the fact that George Orwell lived in the village as a boy, for about three years, and made his first appearance in print with a poem published in the local *Henley and South Oxfordshire Standard* under the only name he had then, Eric Blair.

Near here is the parish of Dunsden and Eye, where there is a Victorian church interesting because it is built of silvery bricks which were made only in the plain at the foot of the hills, where the clay is rich in lime and devoid of iron. This brick can also be seen in the Hare and Hounds Inn at Watlington.

Following the river upstream brings us to Caversham, which is in Berkshire and is separated from Reading only by the river. Although some Chiltern writers include the Cookham area opposite Marlow, Caversham is really the only part of Berkshire that can lay reasonable claim to be in Chiltern country. Whether the Chilterns are anxious to claim Caversham is another matter. It is unbelievably dreary suburbia and gives the unsuspecting visitor every incentive to move on quickly to Mapledurham.

Only a narrow winding lane leads down to this riverside hamlet nestling below the wooded hills, but at the end of it is one of the most rewarding scenes in the Chiltern region, with the Elizabethan mansion and the church standing close to the oldest surviving water-mill on the entire length of the Thames. Mapledurham House was built by Sir Michael Blount and still belongs to his family's descendants – a lovely mellow red-brick building with tall chimneys, gables and oriel windows. The Blounts were a Roman Catholic family and had a small Catholic chapel in the Protestant church, where their monuments remain, although a private chapel was subsequently built in the house.

The vicarage is much more recent and is only of interest because it was erected by a vicar who spent twenty-five years here and is buried in the churchyard – Lord Augustus FitzClarence, one of the offspring of King William IV and the actress Mrs Jordan.

The chief fame of Mapledurham, however, rests on its association with another Catholic, Alexander Pope. Deformed by curvature of the spine, Pope was only four-and-a-half feet tall, understandably over-sensitive, venomous and vindictive, but his brilliance as wit and poet brought him many admirers, among whom were the Blount sisters of Mapledurham, Martha and Theresa. Pope visited the house on a number of occasions, and there is no doubt that he cherished an undeclared love for Martha, with whom he corresponded throughout his life and about whom he wrote the often quoted lines, when she left London for Mapledurham (with slightly resentful humour, for Pope was no country-lover):

> She went to plain-work, and to purling brooks,
> Old-fashioned halls, dull aunts, and croaking rooks.
> She went from Op'ra, park, assembly, play,
> To morning-walks, and pray'rs three hours a day,
> To part her time 'twixt reading and bohea,

The watermill, Mapledurham. Said to be the oldest surviving mill on the River Thames, parts of it date from the fifteenth century. It is in the grounds of Mapledurham House, still owned by descendants of the Blount family whom Pope visited here.

> To muse, and spill her solitary tea,
> Or o'er cold coffee trifle with the spoon,
> Count the slow clock and dine exact at noon.

When Pope was on his death-bed, Martha refused to visit him, but he left her his books and a thousand pounds. "Blessed is the man who expects nothing," he had once written, "for he shall never be disappointed."

If it should occur to the reader that, whilst we may be less than twenty miles from 'The Pink and Lily', we seem a hell of a long way from Rupert Brooke, there is some truth in this. The actual landscape of the Oxfordshire Chilterns is all of a piece with the rest, but, as one approaches the Thames, there is a difference of social and religious development that makes itself felt here. It is partly due to the fact that the luxuriant woodland and the more hospitable country along the valley meant earlier settlement here, and development on more orthodox lines in the Middle Ages, to which the divines of Oxford University also contributed. The very conservative status of the valley has gone hand-in-hand with the area's obvious attractions for the well-to-do of London and elsewhere. It may not have escaped the reader's notice that we have come across Roman Catholics more in this part of the region, and that is not mere coincidence. The Chilterns as a refuge for Protestant heretics began in the more remote country away from the river valley, but, paradoxically, they were a refuge here for the opposite camp, to some extent, when allegiance to Rome was not looked upon with favour in London. Oxfordshire has, for many centuries, had a larger number of Catholic residents than Buckinghamshire and Hertfordshire.

Whitchurch is the next village along our side of the river, and a very attractive one it is, too. It was the birthplace of Sir John Soane, the architect who built the first Bank of England and who left the museum named after him in London. The church contains brasses to Thomas Walysch and his wife, who died in the fifteenth century, he being the wine-taster to the Royal Household.

The River Thames flows gracefully between Whitchurch and Pangbourne, on the opposite bank, and comes finally (as far as we

are concerned) to Goring. The town and its situation are picturesque, with steep hillsides, covered in beech and juniper, rising
from the opposite bank, and a lock and weir on the river. Flowing
through the narrow gap in the chalk ridge, the river here marks the
end of the Chiltern Hills, and, somewhere near here, the Icknield
Way crossed the river by a ford to join the Berkshire Downs.

The Upper Icknield Way near Whiteleaf. The ancient track clearly shows the chalk surface, where it skirts Princes Risborough before rejoining the made-up roadway. Whiteleaf Cross is on the hillside above it.

CHAPTER 5

THE ONCE
AND FUTURE CHILTERNS

SAM JOHNSON, INVITED to admire mountain scenery, denied any grandeur to the spectacle of what he was pleased to call "mere elevated bodies". One suspects he was jealous of something he could not flatten with one of his pompous rejoinders. Hills and mountains can be intimidating, as both Ruskin and Wordsworth discovered in the Lake District, but they are a continually unfolding drama, written by Nature, in which Man plays but a minor role. Johnson had a declared preference for "a furlong of Cheapside", where men have not only written the script but also built the stage, painted the scenery and provided the cast – amateurs, all!

Dr Johnson's ghost has found an unexpected modern ally in Professor W.G. Hoskins, who has pioneered the study of landscape history and finds man-made landscapes superior to natural ones, which he has called "mere scenery".

It seems to me that this philosophy is a somewhat inauspicious one for the future of mankind. That we have created God in the image of Man is witness enough to our megalomania, and madmen will believe anything that suits them. Soon we shall be convinced that what we have always deplored as being ugly is really quite beautiful. The process which has been steadily gathering momentum in many aspects of our lives is now being applied to the landscape – a system of rationalization leading us to approve, or at any rate justify, what we have done for blind economic reasons. It seems to me that we are in desperate need of a little humility in our attitude to nature.

For this reason I find myself, rather reluctantly, on the same side of the fence as H.J. Massingham, the only notable writer on the Chilterns whose intimate knowledge of their life and character can be compared with, say, Wordsworth's of the Lake District. Born in London, Massingham became a journalist like his father and was quite at home in the city until his late thirties, when he underwent what can only be called a conversion to country life. Eventually building a house at Long Crendon, he settled there to write about the English countryside in the tradition of Cobbett and W.H. Hudson. "Love of the country is no longer the prerogative of poets," he wrote, "and has indeed so inundated the general run of people that it is partly responsible for rural desecration."

Until his death in 1952, Massingham immersed himself deeply in English rural traditions and poured out a string of books in which he raged against the disastrous effects of so-called progress since the Industrial Revolution, and, in so doing, changed himself from a young, free-thinking progressive liberal into an old, pessimistic Christian reactionary. The loss of a leg, following a series of accidents, may have been a contributing factor to his view of things.

There can be no doubt that a great deal of what Massingham said about the Chilterns was right, although he was generally regarded as an eccentric who wanted to turn the clock back, who saw good in everything old and evil in most that was new. He echoed Cobbett's dismay (of 1829) at finding straw-plaiters at Tring importing straw from Italy instead of growing it in their own fields, and despaired that a century later we were importing apples from Canada, wool from Australia and mutton from New Zealand, whilst English apples lay rotting on the ground and English sheepwalks were deserted. It is impossible to disagree with Massingham when he deplores the disappearance of traditional English crafts, forced out of existence by mass-production – "sheer murder by evil economics". And one can only cheer at his protest when,

Turville and its valley from Turville Hill: the view from near the converted smock-mill which stands like a sentinel over one of the prettiest of Chiltern villages.

The escarpment from the Lower Icknield Way, near Watlington: the sharp rise of the Chilterns from the Oxfordshire plain, seen as one approaches from the west. The gap is emphasized by a deep cutting made for the M40 motorway.

admiring the trees of Burnham Beeches, he suddenly sees "an iron basket for litter, and a few minutes' walk away is Teashop Road and Cafeteria Corner. The appalling triviality of our civilization hits you like a blow. . . . Did those trees sweat in growth and bulge in form that the travail of earth's beginnings should produce Slough at the end of it?"

Yet, in the very act of cheering Massingham, one recoils from the almost hysterical extremism of some of his views. What he had once embraced, he now attacked with all the unreasonable fanaticism of a typical convert. It is sometimes necessary to overstate a case before anyone will listen to it, but Massingham lost all sense of proportion. Can one reasonably decry the "brutish insensibility" of modern life and at the same time admire the village green at Aldbury without comment on the barbarous use of stocks and whipping-post, where perhaps some mentally defective villager was flogged until the blood ran down his back, for stealing a loaf of bread or consorting with gypsies? And is it not plainly neurotic to liken the ivy clinging on the walls of the ruined church at Bix Bottom to a stoat sucking a rabbit's throat, a python crushing the bones of its prey, and Germany crushing Poland? (Massingham's book *Chiltern Country* was published in 1940.)

Are we already in danger of imagining straw-plaiting as a picturesque English village craft? It was learned by women and children in the Chiltern villages to supplement the pittance the menfolk earned by working in the fields. We have the autobiography of a woman, born at Tring and brought up in the workhouse, who – as a child of twelve – was made by her employer to produce "five yards of straw-plait every night after I had done work at the silkmill. But I had a very good time there. I don't ever remember one of them raising a hand to strike me." Let us not try to romanticize that, or the lace-makers who grew deformed and diseased from their cramped postures in tiny, badly-lit cottages, earning a shilling a day while their husbands worked alone in the woods or on the farms and died of the 'bloody flux' and from other bluntly-named causes, for lack of medical attention.

Massingham saw the Industrial Revolution as a great ogre which fathered on the pure and virginal Chilterns the monstrous progeny of the twentieth century. Even in 1934 he was complaining of "an island so congested with cars that you wonder it does not sink with their weight under the sea". But ugliness and decadence did not suddenly take the stage in the eighteenth and nineteenth centuries. In the first chapter of this book we were already concerned with changes that Man had brought to the landscape. 'Natural' might seem only a relative term when we are talking about any landscape inhabited by humanity. But the self-preservation of Man himself is as natural as any other aspect of life on earth. The pity is always that our wisdom does not match our enterprise.

One can convincingly trace the beginnings of declining standards to Puritanism, or to the Roman occupation, or even (if one is so inclined) to the Garden of Eden. There is a telling line in Tacitus regarding the submission of the ancient Britons to Roman methods and culture: ". . . they gradually deviated into a taste for those luxuries which stimulate to vice; porticos, and baths, and the elegance of the table; and this, from their inexperience, they termed politeness, whilst in reality, it constituted a part of their subservience." In other words, civilization is slavery. But realizing it cannot stop it. Evolution cannot be held in abeyance, even when it is a road to dusty death. We progress through agonies of trial and error, but

we do progress. It is sometimes decades before we can see clearly
that we took a wrong turn, and by that time it is often too late to
change course – we have to make the best of it. But if we did not
use the brains that we, alone among all living things on earth, have
developed to give us the power of choice and judgement and
learning from our past errors, those Chiltern men who were
burned at the stake or branded on their cheeks with red-hot irons
for their conscientious objection, would be mockeries of all human
life.

Massingham, however, saw all progress as delusion and disaster.
It was all very well for him to call High Wycombe a "vast dustbin
of houses", but I do not recall his advocating the banning of sexual
intercourse on pain of death, so that the population could be
reduced and house-building become unnecessary. Yet what alternative is there? Life implies growth, and growth – decay and
death. If urbanization and industry had been entirely withheld
from the Chilterns, they would only have become once again the
"deserts of Chiltern" they were when the Romans had gone – an
uninhabited graveyard of rural England.

Those of us who remember seeing men labouring in the fields
with teams of great horses – their glittering brasses and polished
martingales testifying to the pride their owners took in them –
may not find the sight of ugly tractors chugging across huge fenced
fields very inspiring, but we do not, presumably, want people
starving to death through agricultural methods too outdated to
cope with increased population, even when that population is an
undiscriminating consumer society which eliminates the pleasures
of the changing seasons with central heating, double glazing and
air-conditioning, to say nothing of deep-freezers that take all the
delights out of spring vegetables and summer fruit by producing
them all the year round.

As it is, the Chilterns are very fortunate compared with many
parts of England. They almost escaped the worst effects of the Industrial Revolution altogether. Parliamentary Enclosure may have
affected them considerably, but they did not have vast factory
communities imposed on them, except in High Wycombe, nor did
a complicated network of canals and railways weave an ugly pat-

Watlington — an old shop front. This is No. 20 Couching Street, dating from 1833 — an interesting survival in a town which could once boast a wealth of rural crafts and trades.

tern across the landscape. One might say the Chilterns have been lucky, if one believes in luck. The country folk themselves do. How else explain the popularity of 'Horseshoes' in the public house names? Wherever three or four are gathered together in that name, there will ale be consumed, more or less within licensing hours.

As the Romans did not consider it necessary to infiltrate the hills to any great extent, neither does the tourist industry. The Thames

Peter the Wild Boy (Northchurch). Found in Hanover, unable to speak any language, he was brought to England by George I.

Mrs Humphry Ward (Aldbury). Her novel *Robert Elsmere* created a sensation by attacking Evangelical Christianity.

Sir George Alexander (Chorleywood), one of the most respected of all actor-managers.

William Penn (Jordans), one of the most famous and influential members of the Society of Friends and founder of Pennsylvania.

Bertram Mills (Chalfont St Giles), the best-known of British travelling circus proprietors.

Eric Gill (Speen), an important modern artist who designed type-faces and postage stamps.

Jerome K. Jerome (Ewelme), famous as the author of Three Men in a Boat, the scene of which is the Thames below the Chilterns.

Sir Basil Liddell Hart (Medmenham), author of the official manual on drill and tactics, and historian of both World Wars.

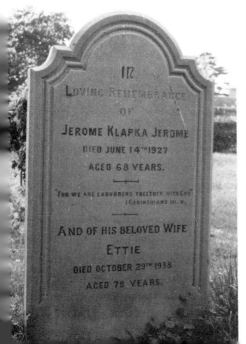

Cow Common, Ewelme: pastoral country near this idyllic Oxfordshire village, seen from Rabbits Hill. It is a scene which has changed very little over the centuries.

and Chilterns Tourist Board, which exists to develop tourism in an area much wider than its name suggests, fortunately concentrates – as far as the Chiltern Hills are concerned – on the great houses and a few isolated curiosities and leaves the quiet villages and hamlets alone. A great deal of Chiltern country, if not 'natural' in the sense of being untouched by human hand, is at least natural in that it is not commercialized or desecrated by industry, and most of it is still best seen on foot, so that it is not yet seriously invaded by that species of modern man who is tethered to his motor-car by an invisible rope only a yard or two long.

People such as he will not endanger the Chiltern countryside except in the more obvious tourist spots. I do not think the ease of transport into the Chilterns is such a threat to their nature as some people imagine. Many a countryman might have been thankful a few years ago that some of the branch railway lines had been taken away, were it not that the M40 had come to take their place. This motorway was strongly opposed by every local group in the Chilterns concerned with the environment, but it came anyway. Have I actually read somewhere that the bridge carrying it over the River Wye is beautiful? As to that, I can only bow to the wisdom of Confucius: "There is beauty in everything, but not everyone sees it." The M40 thrusts its urgent route through the hills like a giant rattlesnake, and it *may* be the thin end of the wedge of development and despoliation, but there are virtually only a couple of exits in the vicinity of High Wycombe before it comes out on the other side of the hills, and I think the motorway may come to be seen as a useful safety valve for the Chilterns, which at least remain relatively free from other hideous manifestations of 'civilization' disfiguring England's not-so-green and sometimes rather unpleasant land – concrete, slag-heaps, rubbish-tips, power-stations, parking-meters, disused railway cuttings, *et al*. Besides, it has to be said that a great deal of the moral outrage of conservationists is

Canning's Oak, Cliveden. Commanding a spectacular view of the famous Cliveden Reach of the Thames, the ancient oak is so named because George Canning used to sit beneath it when he was a guest at Cliveden, now one of the main tourist attractions of the Chilterns.

typical English hypocrisy. The people who make emotional pro-
tests about the quality of life when a new road development is proposed usually have cars in their garages and television aerials on
their roofs, and they, too, want electricity carried to them by
pylons which so often ruin the hilltop views and new convenient
schools where their children can be educated.

Personally, I would whole-heartedly support any road scheme
which had as its object the diversion of the traffic through Amersham and Beaconsfield (I mean the old towns, of course − new
towns get the traffic they deserve).

There is also still − despite commuter growth − a relative scarcity of other 'civilizing' influences. Theatres, cinemas, colleges,
department-stores, multi-storey car-parks, stadiums, discothèques,
even hotels, blocks of flats and the inevitable accompaniments of
all these benefits − mental hospitals − have not penetrated the hills
to any significant extent, and one must go to Aylesbury or Oxford,
Reading, Watford or Luton for them. The Chilterns have not
thrown in the towel in their resistance to exploitation − not by a
long chalk.

The narrow lanes that weave in and out of the villages and hamlets are the chief protectors of the Chiltern character; the most
powerful weapon in the region's armoury of defence against the
marauding motor-car. It is not merely that they are so narrow (the
sign saying "Single track road with passing places" will be familiar
to all but the most cursory of Chiltern motorists); they are also baf-
fling, as if these old tracks between farms and hamlets were delib-
erately made to defeat anyone who might wish to hurry
somewhere, though 'Hard-to-Find Farm' near Flackwell Heath
does admittedly seem a misnomer now that the motorway runs
right by it. The driver who flatters himself that he has an infallible
sense of direction will not easily find his way through these lanes
without a map-reader at his side. Bordered in May and June by
nature's finest ornament, the cow parsley which is surely the most
landscape-enhancing of all British wild flowers, like the lace
edging a silken pillow (not the later hedge parsley − a lady of less
refinement and more doubtful virtue), these lanes are as crafty as
hunted foxes, turning back on themselves and putting up no scent

Landscape near Radnage. Looking west only a few yards from the door of the village church, this peaceful scene is typical of the best Chiltern countryside.

for the pursuers. After all, the natives *know* their way about, and who else but a fool would come to Pishill Bank and want to know the way to Chambersgreen?

The Chiltern Hills have rightly been designated an Area of Outstanding Natural Beauty, but they have not so far acquired the appendages that usually accompany such distinction — camping sites, tourist information centres, hostels. No doubt this situation will change in the foreseeable future. The human responsibility, surely, is not to prevent change or impede it by throwing tantrums at public meetings or by lying down in front of excavators, but to argue earnestly for balance and restraint in the imposition of modernism on this unique part of Britain. Massingham's raging against the delusion of progress was justified in this sense: that we shall be held responsible by future generations for not recognizing the point at which things were allowed to go too far, ruining the quality of the English landscape for our own selfish ends, beyond

Chipperfield – the village school. Children such as these, going unwillingly or otherwise to the old flint school overlooking Chipperfield Common, will inherit the Chilterns we leave for them to enjoy.

redemption. Do not let us give our descendants cause to look back in anger at our blindness.

"What, then, is to become of the Chiltern Hills in the future, young man?"

"Madam, I am flattered that you have stayed with us thus far, but frankly, your guess is as good as mine."

They may become a vast leisure-ground for London and the Home Counties; or merely a more heavily populated commuter area, as the affluent society continues to flee from increasing city stress; they may be cleared of trees and transformed by modern agricultural science into fertile land for growing acres of soya beans to feed the people of the dread city of Milton Keynes. Worst of all, they might be turned by deranged conservationists into a sort of hideous museum of rural life, with a handful of surviving natives sitting around on Windsor chairs and dressed up in smocks and breeches for the tourists' photographs.

We have to be aware of small signs, for changes creep up on us gradually, little by little. If Orwell's deadly vision of 1984 should come to pass, it will not suddenly explode upon us like a bomb on the last day of December 1983. We have already resigned ourselves to some of its heralds, as I discovered when I wandered up a country footpath to take a photograph of Chequers. We accept too much, too soon. This is not a country of revolutions because there is no need for it to be. If those who want change are only a little patient, they can get their way without the apathetic mass of the people noticing that anything has happened, as long as they have their bread and circuses. Although I do not believe in extremism of any sort, therefore, I think it is right that local people everywhere, like the Chiltern inhabitants, should fight to preserve what they cherish, and prevent, if they can, that further standardization and despoliation that takes place at the hands of city men in Whitehall, in whom we should take care never to put *all* our national trust.

Whatever *does* happen to the Chilterns, I hope, for my part, that their spirit will remain in the collective unconscious of the people, infecting their lives with that little touch of magic that distinguishes them subtly from their neighbours to north, south, east and west, and which is the unique and surely indestructible heritage of Chiltern life.

LIST OF SOURCES

B.J. Bailey, *Ashridge Observed* (Inglenook Press, 1975)
    Portrait of Hertfordshire (Robert Hale, 1978)
Dudley Barker, *G.K. Chesterton* (Constable, 1973)
Edmund Blunden, *Shelley – A Life Story* (Collins, 1946)
F.G. Brabant, *Oxfordshire* (Little Guide) (Methuen, 1906)
John Burnett (ed.), *Useful Toil* (Allen Lane, 1974)
John Camp, *Portrait of Buckinghamshire* (Robert Hale, 1972)
William Cobbett, *Rural Rides* (Everyman's Library edition, 1973)
G.R. Crosher, *Along the Chiltern Ways* (Cassell, 1973)
Elizabeth Cull, *Walks Along the Ridgeway* (Spurbooks, 1977)
Daniel Defoe, *A Tour Through the Whole Island of Great Britain* (Penguin
    edition, 1971)
Kevin Fitzgerald, *The Chilterns* (Batsford, 1972)
Michael Foot, *Aneurin Bevan*, Vol. II (Davis-Poynter, 1973)
Paul Hair (ed.), *Before the Bawdy Court* (Elek, 1972)
David and Joan Hay, *Hilltop Villages of the Chilterns* (Phillimore & Cox, 1971)
Sean Jennett, *The Ridgeway Path* (HMSO, 1976)
Ludovic Kennedy, *The Trial of Stephen Ward* (Gollancz, 1964)
Elizabeth Langhorne, *Nancy Astor and Her Friends* (Arthur Barker, 1974)
Donald McCormick, *The Hell-Fire Club* (Jarrolds, 1958)
H.J. Massingham, *Chiltern Country* (Batsford, 1940)
Arthur Mee, *The King's England: Buckinghamshire* (Hodder & Stoughton, 1937)
    The King's England: Oxfordshire (Hodder & Stoughton, 1949)
Nikolaus Pevsner, *The Buildings of England: Hertfordshire* (Penguin, 1953)
    The Buildings of England: Buckinghamshire (Penguin, 1960)
    and Jennifer Sherwood, *The Buildings of England: Oxfordshire* (Penguin,
    1974)
Tacitus, *The Annals of Imperial Rome* (Penguin edition, 1956)
Alison Uttley, *Buckinghamshire* (The County Books) (Robert Hale, 1950)
Victoria County History of Buckinghamshire, Vols. II and III (London, 1925 and
    1969)
Victoria County History of Oxfordshire, Vol. VIII (Oxford University Press, 1964)

INDEX